Autism and It's History in Education - An Outline of Past and Current Effective Educational Options

Regina V. Mignano

Copyright ©1998, 2010 Regina Varin-Mignano – All rights reserved.

No part of this publication either text or image may be used for any purpose other than personal use, except as permitted under Section 107 or 108 under the 1976 United States Copyright act. Therefore, reproduction, modification, storage in a retrieval system or retransmission, in any form or by any means, electronic, mechanical
or otherwise, for reasons other than personal use, is strictly prohibited without prior written permission.

ISBN/EAN13: 9781452817491
Page Count: 127
Binding Type: US Trade Paper
Trim Size: 5"x8""
Language: English
Color: Black and White
Related Categories: Education / Philosophy & Social Aspects

For Christopher, Michael and Paul

Special thanks to Yolanda Vitulli and the staff at Tender Care Human Services, Inc, and all the families and consumers with whom I have interacted over the years. You were my inspiration to write this book.

TABLE OF CONTENTS

*AUTISM - POPULATION DEFINTION &
CHARACTERISTICS
Page 9*

*PAST AND PRESENT POLICY
Page 17*

*A.B.A. AND T.E.A.C.H. – A COMPARISON
Page 27*

*POLICY RECOMMENDATIONS:
Page 35*

*EDUCATIONAL INTERVENTIONS AND THE BIO-
PSYCHO-SOCIAL IMPACT: A REFLECTION
Page 43*

*FOR EVERYONES LIBRARY -A LIST OF BOOKS ON
AUTISM
Page 61*

*BIBLIOGRAPHY
Page 121*

AUTISM - POPULATION DEFINTION & CHARACTERISTICS

~~~~~~~~~~~~~~~~~~~~~~~~~~~~~

The Pervasive Developmental Disorders (or PDD) are a group of psychiatric conditions in which expected social skills, language development, and normal childhood behaviors do not develop appropriately. In general, PDD affects multiple areas of development, are manifested early in life, and cause persistent dysfunction.

Autistic disorder, the best known of the disorders, is characterized by sustained impairment in reciprocal social interactions, communications and stereotypical behavioral patterns. (Kaplan, 1994) Infantile autism was a term coined by Leo Kanner in 1943 but it was not until 1980, in the third edition of the DSM that autistic disorder was recognized as a distinct clinical entity. Kanner suspected the syndrome to be more frequent than it seemed and suggested that some children had been misclassified as mentally retarded or with childhood schizophrenia. (Kaplan, 1994) However, in Kanner's research, he described that these children had exceptional, almost savant-like, rote memory and normal physical appearance. Kanner concluded that these children were capable of achieving normal cognitive abilities. Historically, it was believed that parents of children with autism were overly intellectual, cold-hearted, and had a limited interest in other people. Until the Mid 1970's, treatment regiments involved helping parents, usually mothers, to become less rejective of their children. (Klinger/ Dawson, 1996) However, that theory was dispelled when Dr. Bernard Rimland and Dr. Eric Schloper argued that the disorder was due to a neurological impairment. In practice, they disputed, psychodynamic theories place so much emphasis on the cold, unloving environment in which an autistic child has been raised causes stress for the parents without obtaining results for the child (Lovaas, 1979). According to the fourth edition of the Diagnostic and Statistical Manual of Mental Disorders (DSM-IV), Autism is now considered a developmental disability that typically appears during the first three years of life. The result of a neurological disorder that affects functioning of the brain, autism and its associated behaviors occur in approximately 2 to 5 cases per 10,000 individuals. Several autism-related disorders are also grouped under the broad heading "Pervasive Developmental Disorder" or PDD: PDD-NOS (pervasive developmental disorder, not otherwise specified),

Asperger's syndrome and Rett's syndrome. These three diagnoses are used differently by professionals to describe individuals who manifest some, but not all, of the autism characteristics. The diagnosis of autism is made when a specified number of characteristics listed in the DSM-IV are present, in ranges inappropriate for the child's age. In contrast, a diagnosis of PDD-NOS may be made when a child exhibits fewer symptoms than in autism, although those symptoms may be exactly the same as a child with an autism diagnosis. Asperger and Rett's syndrome display the most marked differences from autism. The following areas are among those that may be affected by autism:

1.) **Communication**: language develops slowly or not at all; use of words without attaching the usual meaning to them; communicates with gestures instead of words; short attention spans

2.) Social Interaction: spends time alone rather than with others; shows little interest in making friends; less responsible to social cues such as eye contact or smiles

3.) **Sensory Impairment**: unusual reactions to physical sensations such as being overly sensitive to touch or under-responsive to pain; sight, hearing, touch, pain, smell, taste may be affected to a lesser or greater degree

4.) Play: lack of spontaneous or imaginative play; does not imitate others actions; doesn't initiate pretend games

5.) Behaviors: may be overactive or very passive; throw frequent tantrums for no apparent reason; may perseverate on a single item, idea or person; apparent lack of common sense; may show aggressive or violent behavior or injure self.

Contrary to popular understanding, many children and adults with autism make eye contact, show affection, smile and laugh, and show a variety of other emotions, but in varying degrees. Like other children, they respond to their environment in positive and negative ways. The autism may affect their range of responses and make it more difficult to control how their body and mind react. They live normal life spans and the behaviors associated with may change or disappear over time. Autism is four times more prevalent in boys than girls and knows no racial, ethnic or social boundaries. Early Studies suggested that a high Socio-Economic status was common in families with autistic children. However, later research shows that family income, lifestyle and educational levels do not affect the chance of autism's occurrence

Autism is known to interfere with the normal development of

the brain in the areas of reasoning, social interaction and communication skills. Children and adults with autism typically have deficiencies in verbal and non-verbal communication, social interactions and leisure or play activities. The disorder makes it hard for them to communicate with others and relate to the outside world. They may exhibit repeated body movements (hand flapping, rocking), unusual responses to people or attachments to objects and resist any changes in routines. In some cases, aggressive and/or self-injurious behavior may be present.

It is conservatively estimated that nearly 400,000 people in the U.S. today have some form of autism. Individuals with autism may have other disorders which affect the functioning of the brain, such as epilepsy, mental retardation, or genetic disorders, such as Fragile X Syndrome. In most cases, there is an associative diagnosis of mental retardation, commonly in the moderate to severe range. (DSM IV, p. 67) Approximately 25-30% may develop a seizure pattern at some period during life. It's prevalence rate now places it as the third most common developmental disability - more common than Down's syndrome. Yet the majority of the public, including many professionals in the medical, educational, and vocational fields are still unaware of how autism affects people and how to effectively work with individuals with autism.

Autism is often referred to as a spectrum disorder, meaning that the symptoms and characteristics of autism can present themselves in a wide variety of combinations, from mild to severe. Although autism is defined by a certain set of behaviors, children and adults can exhibit any combination of the behaviors in any degree of severity. Two children, both with a diagnosis of autism, can act very differently from one another.

Medical researchers are exploring different explanations for the various forms of autism. Although one specific cause of autism is not known, current research links autism to biological or neurological differences in the brain. MRI (Magnetic Resonance Imaging) and PET (Positron Emission Topography) scans show abnormalities in the structure of the brain, with significant differences within the cerebellum, including the size and number of Purkinje cells. In some families there appears to be a pattern of autism or related disabilities, which suggests there may be a genetic basis to the disorder, although at this time no one gene has been directly linked to autism. A wide range of pre, peri, and post-natal conditions are thought to pre-dispose children to the development of autism, including maternal rubella, untreated fetal phenyuletunora, tuberous sclerosis, anoxia during birth, encephalitis, infantile spasms and fragile X Syndrome. (Moroz, 1989)

There are no medical tests for diagnosing autism. A diagnosis is mainly based on observations of the child's communication, behavior and developmental levels. However, because many of the behaviors associated with autism are shared by other disorders, a doctor may complete various medical tests to rule out other possible causes.

Below are several diagnostic tools have been developed over the past few years to help professionals make an accurate autism diagnosis:

CHAT - Checklist for Autism in Toddlers

CARS - Childhood Autism Rating Scale

PIA - Parent Interviews for Autism

GARS - Gilliam Autism Rating Scale

BRIAC - Behavior Rating Instrument for Autistic and other Atypical Children

(Kaplan, 1994.)

A brief observation in a single setting cannot present a true picture of an individual's abilities and behaviors. At first glance, the person with autism may appear to have mental retardation, a behavior disorder, or even problems with hearing. However, it is important also to distinguish autism from other conditions, since an accurate diagnosis can provide the basis for building an appropriate and effective educational and treatment program.

There are great differences among people with autism. Some individuals mildly affected may exhibit only slight delays in language and greater challenges with social interactions. They may have average or above average verbal, memory or spatial skills but find it difficult to be imaginative or join in a game of softball with their friends. Others more severely affected may need greater assistance in handling day to day activities like crossing the street or making a purchase.

PAST AND PRESENT POLICY

Historically, governmental policy surrounding Autism has been one of institutionalization. Ninety-five percent of persons with autism lived in institutions because of lack of alternative educational and human services, at least until 1976. (Moroz, p.113) As a group, children and youths with autism are the population most at risk in the United States for institutionalization due to their specific behaviors. Most children and adults with autism received their primary education and needs in institutions until the early 1970's, when deinsutionalization and the increase in availability of psychiatric medications took effect. Prior to that, persons with severe and persistent mental disorders were generally cared for in state hospitals. (Grob, 1993) If admitted in their youth, as with many autistic, they often remained institutionalized for decades. After 1970, the mentally disabled's care came under the jurisdiction of a series of federal entitlement programs, which presumed that income payments would enable persons to live in the community. With the autistic population, however, most were moved into community residences, developmental centers, or returned home. The guiding theory of the deinstutionalization of the developmentally disabled population became that of integration and normalization. An example of this is the Willowbrook Decree of New York State. Former Governor Hugh L. Carey signed this decree in 1975 to "Provide safe, attractive, comfortable and homelike environments in which more personalized care is delivered to the severely mentally disabled and retarded (CQC, 1982.) This decree grew out of strong convictions about the negative qualities of large segregated, custodial institutions and the right of the disabled individual to grow and develop as members of their own community. In New York State, the care of the Autistic and Developmentally Disabled was then put into the care of the New York State Office of Mental Retardation and Developmental Disabilities. Many mentally disabled individuals, through this office, were then placed into the community into care facilities, conversely to save the Federal and State Government money. In a 1979 study of facilities in New York, the estimated yearly costs of institutional care to be $14,700 annually, compared with $9300 - $11,000 annually for group home care (Spano, 1987.) In 1982, the average annual cost per resident in a community residence increased to $28,639 annually, compared to an annual per client cost of $37,024 per client in a Developmental Center or an institution. (CQC, 1982) For those that lived at home, Federal entitlements, such as Supplemental Security Income (SSI), food stamps, and Medicaid helped defray the costs of living at home. Currently, a Developmentally Disabled child diagnosed as autistic is eligible for SSI payments of up to $469.00 per month plus Medicaid benefits, and an adults about $565.00 per month. However, the autistic individual is not classified into its own sub-category. According to the Social Security Administration, if the autistic individual has an IQ of under 75, they are classified as mentally retarded. If over 75, they are considered emotionally disturbed or other mental disorders. (SSA-1997). The mentally retarded classification, therefore, would effect approximately 75% of the autistic population. These two categories compromise 27.8% an 29.9% of the population, respectively (see Appendix A – 7.F and 7.A SSI: Disability).

While no one can predict the future, we do know that some adults with autism live and work independently in the community, while others depend on the support of family and professionals. Adults with autism can benefit from vocational training to provide them with the skills needed for obtaining jobs, in addition to social and recreational programs. Adults with autism may live in a variety of residential settings, ranging from independent home or apartments to group homes, supervised apartment settings, living with other family members to more structured residential care.

In addition to the deinstutionalization of the autistic and mentally disabled population came the need for abundant and appropriate educational placement. Historically, disabled (and autistic) children were removed from regular classrooms and placed in special classes, home teaching, private schools or institutions. However, with the movement towards deinstutionalization, there became a need for more special education programs in a time where they were few around and waiting lists for others.

For Example, in New York State (a progressive state in special education services) a 1944 law declared that the Education Department should "stimulate all private and public efforts designed to relieve, care for, cure or educate physically handicapped children," and coordinate its efforts with other governmental programs. This policy statement was extended in 1957 to include mentally retarded children as well. Ten years later the "handicapped child" was legally, and more flexibly, redefined as an individual who "because of mental, physical or emotional reasons, cannot be educated in regular classes but can benefit by special services and programs." (Data Research, 1997) This definition summarized New York State policy, which since the early years of the century had favored removing handicapped children from regular classrooms and schools, and placing them in "special classes," home teaching, or private schools.

In the 1950s and '60s this policy began to shift toward "inclusion." Public schools were authorized to hold special classes for severely mentally handicapped children starting 1955, and required to do so after 1961. During the 1960s the New York State Department of Education encouraged efforts to place multi-handicapped or brain-injured children in public schools. Special aid to schools for education of handicapped children, abolished in 1962, was restored by legislative acts in 1974 and 1976. A broad-ranging Regents policy statement on "Education of Children with Handicapping Conditions" in 1973 recommended placing them in regular classrooms when possible. School committees on the handicapped were required by a Commissioner's regulation. In 1977 the Commissioner ordered the New York City school system to improve its special education programs, which had long waiting lists and many unserved children. Federal aid for new programs to educate children with handicapping conditions was authorized under the ESEA Title VI-A in 1967. Congress passed the Education of All Handicapped Children Act in 1975 (revised in 1990 and again in 1997 as the Individuals with Disabilities Education Act, IDEA). This federal act required the states to provide all children with disabilities with a "free, appropriate education in the least restrictive environment. However, minimal federal aid (about 9% of all funding) came with this big mandate. Therefore the state and the local governments were required to pick up the other 91% of the tab. A 1976 state law required the school committees on special education to develop an individualized educational program in the "least restrictive environment, After the mid-1970s, most New York State school districts were responsible for recommending and providing services for all children of school age who were identified as having disabilities.

A method under the IDEA to involve parents in their child's educational plan is the development of the Individualized Educational Program (IEP). The IEP is the cornerstone for the education of a child with a disability. The IEP is a written statement of a child's educational program, which identifies the services a child needs so that he or she may grow and learn during the school year. The IEP outlines the child's special education plan by defining goals for the school year, services needed to help the child meet those goals, and a method of evaluating the student's progress. As its name suggests, the Individualized Educational Program should be written to reflect the child's individual and unique needs. Accordingly, no single IEP would be appropriate for all children with autism. Under explicit provisions of P.L. 105-17 which are effective July 1st 1998, Parents must be included in the IEP team (Sec. 614 (d)(1)(B)). Additionally with the 1997 Reauthorization of IDEA, parents must now be included as "members of any group that makes decisions on the educational placement of the child" (Sec. 614 (f)). Parents may bring a list of suggested goals and objectives, as well as additional information that may be pertinent, to the IEP meeting.

Under the IEDA Section PL 94-142, Autism was categorized as a "severe emotional disturbance." Although this was eventually changed at the federal level to a subcategory under other health impaired in 1981, autism still was categorized as an emotional disturbance for educational purposes in many parts of the U.S. (Moroz, p.108) It wasn't until 1990 that the IDEA, under its revisions, saw Autism as a separate and distinct category. Therefore, much data relating to the education and service of autistic children is limited to only a few years. However, the number of school aged autistic children served in the United States under the IEDA significantly increased by 19.5% alone between 1993-1995, as compared to other disabilities (see Appendix B). The significant increase is due, in part, to the new research and increased awareness tot he autistic diagnosis.

For most autistic children, educational management should emphasize development of social skills and communicative language. The long-term goal should be to permit the child to function as effectively and comfortably as possible in the least restrictive environment. (Bauer, 1993) But the majority of autistic children in special education classrooms are unable to move into "less restrictive environments" due to their disruptive behaviors. This is due, in part, to the education of professions about autism – which has been reportedly slow. As stated earlier, autistic children were clumped together with children with "serious emotional disturbances." Most public school teachers in the field of autism, according to Munoz, had received training in emotional disturbances, learning disabilities, behavior disorders, or some other category of students less severely impaired than children with autism (p. 113.) Many teachers also reported feeling poorly prepared to work with the autistic children in the classroom. In New York City, for example, children with autism are grouped under an

"Autistic" category and are regulated to a specialized Instructional Environment (SIE – III) – segregated from the mainstream population. Autistic children in the SIE-III units are in a classroom of a 6:1:1 student-teacher ratio, with individualized support services of speech, occupational, and physical therapy as deemed appropriate. However, due to lack of training with this population, the teachers use a curriculum focused on "life skills" and little to no intervention for their maladaptive or disruptive behaviors. Furthermore, the autistic child in this SIE-III unit is restricted from the chance of being integrated into a less restrictive environment by physically being separated from regular or higher functioning disabled children.

APPLIED BEHAVIOR ANALYSIS AND T.E.A.C.H. : A COMPARISON

There are many different types of therapeutic programs offered in private school and therapeutic settings. Two of the most effective programs proven to work effectively is the statewide program in North Carolina, developed by Dr. Eric Schloper, Dr. Meisbov, and associates at division TEACCH at the University of North Carolina. The longitudinal study of early intensive behavioral treatment of autistic children by Dr. O. Ivar Lovaas in California is the second. What are the cost benefits to each of these programs, compared to the traditional methods used at present? It is important to examine and compare each program specifically to its teaching method, success rate, and monetary cost to run it. It is also important to examine the in-tangential benefits that come with each program (e.g.: an autistic individual possibly becoming a productive member in society) and measure the benefits of each program to the movement of the autistic child.

The first program that I will discuss is the Lovaas style

Intensive behavioral treatment program founded by Dr. O. Ivar Lovaas from the University of California, Loss Angeles. It is argued (Lovaas, 1979) that behavior modification is the most effective form of intervention in the treatment of autism. This method focuses on the elimination of the many maladaptive behaviors demonstrated by autistic children. It also includes the broadening the behavioral repertoire to include more adaptive patterns of behavior (Waters, 1990) The various procedures employed to increase behavior are generally based on the operant principles of reinforcement for desires behavior while maladaptive behaviors can be decreased through the use on consequences. This viewpoint is based on the idea that the different autistic behaviors might be related to several different kinds of antecedent conditions. One characteristic of autistic children is that they express little emotion. These behaviors are, it is argued (Lovaas, 1979), left largely unaltered because they are not well understood and therefore not taught. The Lovaas model is notable because of the striking results that are claimed for it, including increase in IQ, educational placement, and adaptive function.

The initial Lovaas treatment program started with young children under four years of age, lasted two years, and was very intensive – requiring one to one staff: child ratio 40 hours per week. The children were then followed over a 5 to 10 year period, which resulted in over 60% of the children either being in less restrictive or general educational settings. The other 40% were in special education settings, but only 15% of those made no significant gains. (Bauer, 1995) For example, a single varied study conducted by Ogletree, Fischer, and Sprouse (1995) focused on an intensive Lovaas-style behavioral treatment plan to stimulate sematic/pragmatic language development in a child with high functioning autism. The independent variable was a treatment sequence emphasizing video vignettes and role-plays. Dependent variables included efficient gaze, responding without delays and topic matience. The study was done over 12 treatment sessions of 45 minutes each twice per week. The results of the study showed a 61% increase in appropriate gaze, a marked increase in topic episodes of appropriate conversational length (47%) but no change in the responses without delays from the baseline sessions. (Ogletree, ET al, 1995) Behavior change through the use of behavior modification is sometimes very slow. Lovaas (1979) commented on the fact that it is hard work to treat autistic people because of the slow rate of response to treatment. This style of behavior modification requires long periods of intensive work, early intervention (pre-school age), and intensive training in order to be successful.

Developed in the early 1970's by Dr. Eric Schopler, the TEACCH (Treatment and Education of Autistic and related Communication Handicapped Children) approach includes a focus on the person with autism and the development of a program around this person's skills, interests, and needs. The major priorities include centering on the individual, understanding autism, adopting appropriate adaptations, and a broadly based intervention strategy building on existing skills and interests. (Meisbov, 1994) By focusing on the individual the person or autistic child becomes the priority, rather than any philosophical notion like inclusion, discrete trial training, facilitated communication, etc. An individualized assessment plan is created to understand the individual better and also "the culture of autism," suggesting that people with autism are part of a distinctive group with common characteristics that are different, but not necessarily inferior, to the rest of society. Emphasizing assessment and the culture of autism requires an understanding of people with autism as they are and to build programs around where each person is functioning.

Structured teaching is an important priority because of the TEACCH research and experience that structure fits the "culture of autism" more effectively. Organizing the physical environment (if by colors, numbers, or other visual cues), developing schedules and work systems, making expectations clear and explicit, and using visual materials have been some effective ways of developing skills and allowing people with autism to use these skills independently of direct adult prompting (as with the Lovaas style program) and cueing. Most programs dealing with developmental disabilities emphasize remediating deficits and focus their entire efforts on that goal. The TEACCH approach, respecting the "culture of autism," recognized that the differences between people with autism and others. (Meisbov, 1994) Their relative strengths in visual skills, recognizing details, and memory, among other areas, can become the basis of successful adult functioning.

The TEACCH approach is also broad-based, taking into account all aspects of the lives of people with autism and their families. Although independent work skills are emphasized, it is also recognized that "life is not all work and that communication, social and leisure skills can be learned by people with autism and can have an important impact on their well-being" (Bauer, 1995.) An important part of the TEACCH curriculum is developing communication skills, pursuing social and leisure interests, and encouraging people with autism to pursue more of these opportunities. In addition to these techniques of understanding autism, developing appropriate structures, promoting independent work skills, emphasizing strengths and interests and fostering communication, social and leisure outlets, the TEACCH approach is most successfully implemented on a systems level. Based on the concept that coordination and integration over time is as important as consistency within a given situation, the TEACCH approach is most effective when it is applied across age groups and agencies. TEACCH believes that the interests of people with autism are best served with coordinated and cooperative programming based on consistent principles over a lifetime. The TEACCH assessment called PEP (Psycho Educational Profile) tries to identify areas where the person "passes", areas where the skill isn't there yet, and areas where the skill is emerging. These domains are then put in an education program for the person. Several outcome studies have examined parent reports of the effectiveness of Structured Teaching and the TEACCH intervention programs Schopler, Meisbov, DeVellis, and Short (1981) received completed questionnaires from 348 families who had participated in the TEACCH program. Parents consistently and with overwhelming enthusiasm, reported that their relationships with Division TEACCH were positive, productive, and enriching. Most impressive were the parents' reports of the high percentage of their adolescent and adult children with autism who were still functioning in community-based programs. Of the families with older children among the respondents, 96% reported that their children were still living in their local communities. This response compared favorably with concurrent follow-up studies showing that between 39% and 74% of autistic adolescents and adults were generally in large residential programs outside of their local communities. The number of clients successfully working in the TEACCH Supported Employment Program is another important outcome measure, perhaps even the most important because it represents the culmination of TEACCH's many intervention activities, early identification, parent training, education, social and leisure skill development, communication training, and vocational preparation. Successful Supported Employment placements are a major goal of many programs serving people with autism and related disabilities. Division TEACCH is using three models of supported Employment: individual competitive placements, dispersed enclaves, and mobile crews. All of these models have clients working a minimum of 15 hours per week earning minimum wage or above with an adult to client supervision ratio of 3:1 or less intensive Supported employment clients earn an average hourly wage of $5.30 working an average if 28 hours per week.

POLICY RECOMMENDATIONS

~~~~~~~~~~~~~~~~~~~~~~~~

Due to the examination of past and current policy provisions with autism, a number of problems in regards to educational movement and placement arose. Therefore, it may be feasible to recommend the following for future policy oriented considerations:

1.) **Education of Teachers**: Due to the nature of autism only recently becoming an educational classification, teachers and other educational professionals should be trained to understand the disorder and its severity. Personnel preparation, according to Munoz (1989), in the field of autism has been inadequate. Not only with teachers, but social workers, school psychologist, residential care, family counselors, and other professionals could benefit from intensive pre-service and in-service training on autism. However, state-programming policies may not be implemented fully unless the proposed interventions are perceived to meet local needs and convictions. (Munoz, p. 114) Community education is also needed to increase awareness of autism. Such efforts could generate support for the development and awareness of services in most communities. These additional services can help families deal with the autistic child's behaviors without judgment and understanding.

2.) **Education of Medical Professionals**: According to Barnett (1995), early intervention with special needs child on a pre-school level can produce large short term benefits for children on their intelligence quotient (IQ), school achievement, grade retention, placement, and social adjustment. It is important that Pediatricians and other medical personnel receive the necessary training in recognizing the symptoms of autism, since they have frequent contact with the child and family. However, few university degree programs prepare professionals to work with autistic children and their families. Early intervention and treatment of autism can significantly decrease many maladaptive behaviors.

Pharmacological management of an autistic child's behaviors can sometimes help decrease them to a more manageable level. A knowledge base of autism can help the pediatrician help the child and the family in a more effective way in this area.

3.) **<u>Programmatic Changes</u>**: Since the Department of education only funds 9% of the cost for Special education, the state and local government are left with paying the majority of the bill (91%). Recently the Department of Education – National Institute on Disability and Rehabilitation Research are advocating for programmatic changes that will focus on children with "severe problem behaviors." The institute feels that physical aggression, violence, and self-injurious behaviors are among the primary obstacles to full inclusion of children and youth with disabilities in age appropriate community-based activities and regular education settings (1997). The department has explored and agreed that these "children" respond best to a structured and non-aversive approach. The current methods, as shown in the *Digest of Education Statistics* (see Appendix), clearly shows the lack of movement of the autistic person to a less restrictive setting. Funding for training and implementation of a Lovaas or TEACCH style method can significantly increase the movement of autistic children to a least restrictive environment. It would also reduce the overall cost of special education due to decreased enrollment in a segregated setting. However, both programs have their drawbacks. For one, the Lovaas Style – intensive behavior modification program, the most statistically successful overall, can also be the most costly and demanding. The state and local Board of Education would have to initially invest more funds to provide a one-to-one student-teacher ratio to make the program most effective. Also, staff would have to provide the teaching and structure of the program to already overwhelmed families. The TEACCH program is less demanding, but there is less long-term research to show a specific movement into a least restrictive environment. Even though many autistic individuals have employment capabilities in adulthood, they still need the supervision of the TEACCH program to carry out these activities. Also, there is no evidence of the autistic individual moving off of an already overused SSI and welfare system. To be effective, an approach should be flexible in nature, rely on positive reinforcement, be re-evaluated on a regular basis and provide a smooth transition from home to school to community environments. A good program will also incorporate training and support systems for the caregivers as well. Rarely can a family, classroom teacher or other caregiver provide effective habilitation for a person with autism unless offered consultation or in-service training by a specialist knowledgeable about the disability. Lastly, students with autism should have training in vocational skills and community living skills at the earliest possible age. Learning to cross a street safely, to make a simple purchase or to ask assistance when needed are critical skills, and may be difficult, even for those with average intelligence levels. Tasks that enhance the person's independence, give more opportunity for personal choice or allow more freedom in the community are important.

4.) **<u>Family Advocacy, Education and Support</u>**: The benefits of involving parents in their children's education are well documented and routinely practiced by school social workers. Family involvement in the education of an autistic child at school and at home becomes more critical because the child's successful development of independent living skills and the family's ability to maintain the young person at home hinges partially on the comprehensiveness and continuity of the child's education (Munoz, 1989). Parents should be taught about the numerous professional supports that are available to them (E.G. Homemaker, respite and child care, transportation.) Parents should also be taught the importance of Behavior Modification and how to become more aware of what is on their child's Individual Education Plan (IEP). Parents must be allowed the option of focusing on their family needs without being blamed for their child's disability.

Our understanding of autism has grown tremendously since it was first described in 1943. Some of the earlier searches for "cures" now seem unrealistic in terms of today's understanding of brain-based disorders. To cure means, "to restore to health, soundness, or normality." In the medical sense, there is no cure for the differences in the brain, which result in autism.

However, we're finding better ways to understand the disorder and help people cope with the various symptoms of the disability. Some of these symptoms may lessen as the child ages; others may disappear altogether. With appropriate intervention, many of the autism behaviors can be positively changed, even to the point that the child or adult may appear to the untrained person to no longer have autism. The majority of children and adults will, however, continue to exhibit some symptoms of autism to some degree throughout their entire lives. A generation ago, 90% of the people with autism were eventually placed in institutions. Today, as a result of appropriate and individualized services and programs, even the more severely disabled can be taught skills to allow them to develop to their fullest potential.

EDUCATIONAL INTERVENTIONS AND THE BIO-PSYCHO-SOCIAL IMPACT: A REFLECTION

According to many experts, intervention at early stages in the child's development may have a greater chance for success for children with autism. Medical, educational, and psychological advancements in the area of autism suggest that the period where the most "curative" treatment can occur is from early intervention through preschool (from age 2-6 years). Most experts agree that intervention at earlier stages in the child's development may have a greater chance of reducing the short-term and long-term negative consequences of these disorders (Guralnick, 1997). Hope for potentially a successful outcome has led, in part, to the increased emphasis on programs for "early intervention" over the past decade.

Behavioral and educational interventions have become the predominant approach for treating children and adults with autism (Bregman and Gerdtz, 1997). In recent years several intensive intervention programs for children with autism have been developed utilizing a systematic behavioral approach, often referred to as *applied behavioral analysis* (ABA). Many of the current forms of speech and language therapy and many other educational interventions for young children with autism are based upon somewhat similar behavioral principles.

Pioneered by Lovaas in UCLA in 1979, behavior modification has been found to be the most effective form of intervention in the treatment of autism. This method focuses on the elimination of the many maladaptive behaviors demonstrated by autistic children. It also includes broadening the behavioral repertoire to include more adaptive patterns of behavior. The Lovaas model is notable because of the striking results that are claimed for it, including increase in IQ, educational placement, and adaptive function.

The initial Lovaas treatment program started with young children under four years of age, lasted two years, and was very intensive. It required a one to one staff: child ratio for 40 hours per week. Lovaas (1979) commented on the fact that it is hard work to treat autistic people because of the slow rate of response to treatment. This style of behavior modification requires long periods of intensive work, early intervention (pre-school age), and intensive training in order to be successful. This intensive treatment and therapeutic services are usually well organized and very supportive up until the child advances to the kindergarten level. At that time, due mostly to budget constraints, a significant portion of these services are no longer available.

During transitional phases, parents and their children with developmental disabilities like autism can experience intense stress. They typically experience the greatest amount of stress when a child with autism encounters a new environment or situation (Stone, Ousley, Hepburn, Hogan, & Brown, 1999). Thus, the transition to a new school or new teacher, or a loss in services for a child with a developmental disability like autism, may be met with a myriad of feelings and behaviors that can create stress for both the parent and the child (Newsome, 2000). The individualization of the child at the preschool level is a preferred model of treatment that focuses on each child's needs. This type of therapeutic service is a support that most parents crave. The transition into school age with its lack of such services leaves them scrambling for additional resources and services on their own.

Biological Aspects:

What causes autism specifically is not known. Some experts believe the cause is biochemical. It is thought to be biological in that it is four times more prevalent in boys than girls. But regardless of gender, autism is known to interfere with the normal development of the brain in the areas of reasoning, social interaction and communication skills. Children and adults with autism typically have deficiencies in verbal and non-verbal communication, social interactions and leisure or play activities. The disorder makes it hard for them to communicate with others and relate to the outside world. They may exhibit repeated body movements (hand flapping, rocking), unusual responses to people or attachments to objects, and resist any changes in routines. In some cases, aggressive and/or self-injurious behavior may be present.

It is conservatively estimated that nearly 400,000 people in the U.S. today have some form of autism. They also may have other disorders that affect the functioning of the brain, such as epilepsy and mental retardation, or genetic disorders such as Fragile X Syndrome. In most cases, including autism, there is an associative diagnosis of mental retardation, commonly in the moderate to severe range (DSM IV-TR, 2001, p. 67). Approximately 25-30% may develop a seizure pattern at some period during life. Autism's prevalence rate is the third most common developmental disability. Yet, the majority of the public, including many professionals in the medical, helping, educational and vocational fields, are still unaware of how autism affects people and how to effectively work with individuals with autism. There are no diagnostic medical tests. A diagnosis is mainly based on observations of the child's communication, behavior and developmental levels. However, because many of the behaviors associated with autism are shared by other disorders, a medical doctor may complete various medical tests to rule out other possible causes.

Because autism is a spectrum disorder, no one method alone is usually effective in treating it. Professionals and families have found that a combination of treatments may be valuable in treating symptoms and behaviors that make it hard for individuals with autism to function. These may include a combination of psychosocial and pharmacological interventions. Although prescribing medications is beyond the purview of social workers, it is important that they become familiar with their purposes and possible side effects. Aman et al.(2003) report in their research that the most commonly prescribed drugs were the antidepressants (fluoxetine, sertraline, fluvoxamine), followed by the neuroleptics (risperidone, olanzapine, thioridazine), antiepileptics (valproicacid, carbamazapine, lamotrigine), antihypertensives (clonidine, propanolol, metoprolol), stimulants (methylphenidate, dextroamphetamine, amphetamine salts), sedative/anxiolytics (melatonin, buspirone, diazepam), and mood stabilizers (valproic acid, carbamazepam, lithium, and others). Forty-five percent of individuals were on one agent and 20% were on two or more psychotropic agents.

Compared with a study 8 to 10 years ago (Aman, Van Bourgondien, Wolford, & Sarphare, 1995), there has been a substantial increase in the use of the SSRIs (266%), antihypertensives (200%), and stimulants (43%). Autism supplements (B6, dimethylglycine, dimethylaminoethanol) have increased by one hundred percent. The investigators highlight limitations in the empirical basis for much of this treatment and the need for research to address these issues and others that affect effective pharmacological treatment. Social workers, for example, frequently deal with compliance issues in the administration of these medications to children, and the parents' acceptance of the need for their child to take these medications. Changes to diet and the addition of certain vitamins or minerals may also help with behavioral issues. According to the Autism Society of America (2004), over the past 10 years, there have been claims that adding essential vitamins such as B6 and B12 and removing gluten and casein from a child's diet may improve digestion, allergies and sociability. Not all researchers and experts agree about whether these therapies are effective or scientifically valid. Clearly, further research is needed.

Psychological Aspects:

Infantile autism was a term coined by Kanner in 1943, but it was not until 1980, in the third edition of the DSM, that autistic disorder was recognized as a distinct clinical entity. Kanner suspected the syndrome to be more frequent than it appeared at the time and suggested that some children had been misclassified as mentally retarded or suffering with childhood schizophrenia (Kaplan, 1994). However, Kanner found that the children in the study had exceptional, almost savant-like, rote memory and normal physical appearance. He concluded that they were capable of achieving normal cognitive abilities. The recent medical and the current psychological research have made great strides over the last 10 years in the survival and security of autistic children and their families. Historically, it was believed that parents of children with autism were overly intellectual, cold-hearted, and had a limited interest in other people. Until the mid 1970's, treatment regimens involved helping parents, usually mothers, to become less rejecting of their children (Klinger/Dawson, 1996). However, that theory was dispelled when Rimland and Schloper researched the disorder in 1984 and found that it was due to a neurological impairment, not poor parenting. In practice, they argued, psychodynamic theories that place so much emphasis on the cold, unloving environment in which an autistic child has been raised caused stress for the parents without obtaining results for the child (Lovaas, 1987).

Despite the disruption of typical learning processes, behavioral scientists have utilized principles and procedures of learning theory to develop effective treatment methodologies for teaching children with autism. In his 1987 follow-up study, Lovaas reported that 17 out of 19 children who received intensive behavioral treatment significantly improved their social, self-help, play and communication skills, including the development of functional speech. Furthermore, 9 of the 19 children were able to successfully complete first grade in regular education classes and were indistinguishable from their peers on measures of IQ, adaptive skills, and emotional functioning. A follow-up study by McEachin, Smith and Lovaas (1993) showed that treatment gains were maintained more than six years later and eight of the children continued to progress in regular education classes without support. All of these behavioral psychologists have influenced the treatment of autistic children markedly.

Social Aspects:

The social problem of autism extends beyond the affected child to those who care for them. Caring for an autistic child can be overwhelming and sometimes almost insurmountable due to the specific behaviors that these children exhibit. Respite care is often difficult if not impossible to obtain, let alone finding a qualified person to manage the child's behaviors. Frustration, anxiety and tension appear to be common feelings reported by mothers of autistic children (Rodrigue, Morgan, and Geffken, 1990). Helping autistic children and their families achieve a sense of belonging in their community are generally not addressed by experts in the field.

Contrary to previous studies, recent research reveals that family income, lifestyle and educational levels do not affect the likelihood of autism's occurrence. However, they do affect familial stress. Patterson (2002) notes that a family's ability to be resilient in the face of normative or significant risk is related not only to their internal relational processes, but also to risks or opportunities in the social systems in their ecological context. Living in poverty and in crime-ridden, violent neighborhoods, for example, place families at high risk and contribute to their inability to satisfactorily accomplish their core functions. Risk processes in the family (such as marital conflict and child abuse) are more likely to emerge under these social conditions. The absence of needed community resources to support families in fulfilling their core functions further undermines family resilience.

Families with an autistic child are particularly vulnerable. Public programs and policies, societal norms and values, and other community institutions, shape the style and degree to which families are able to fulfill their functions, as well as their ability to acquire and develop new capabilities when challenged. As a group, due to their specific behaviors, children and youth with autism are the population most at risk in the United States for institutionalization. Under the IEDA Section PL 94-142 (1996), autism was categorized as a "severe emotional disturbance." Although this was eventually changed and categorized as "other health impaired" in 1981, autism still was categorized as an emotional disturbance for educational purposes in many parts of the U.S. (Moroz, 1989, p.108). It wasn't until 1990 that the IDEA was revised to categorize autism as separate and distinct. Consequently, much of the data relating to the education and service for autistic children is limited to only a few years. However, due in part to the new research and increased awareness of the autistic diagnosis, the reported number of school aged autistic children served in the United States under the IEDA significantly increased by 19.5% alone between 1993-1995, as compared to other disabilities.

For most autistic children, educational management should emphasize the development of social skills and communicative language. The long-term goal should be to permit the child to function as effectively and comfortably as possible in the least restrictive environment (Bauer, 1993). The problem is that the majority of autistic children in special education classrooms are unable to move into "less restrictive environments" due to their disruptive behaviors. This is due, in part, to the education of professions about autism – which has been reportedly slow. Too often, autistic children are still grouped together with children with "serious emotional disturbances." Most public school teachers and ancillary professionals in the field of autism - such as social workers, according to Moroz (1989), had received training in emotional disturbances, learning disabilities, behavior disorders, or some other category of students less severely impaired than children with autism (p. 113.) Many social workers also reported feeling poorly prepared to work with the autistic children and their families.

There is little doubt that parenting a child with autism is extremely demanding due to the relatively poor diagnostic understanding by the general public when compared with other disabilities such as Down Syndrome (Fisman, Wolf, & Noh, 1989), the consequent marked antipathy for the typical behavior exhibited by children with autism (Koegel et al., 1992), and also because of the socially inappropriate and aggressive nature of much autistic behavior. Not surprisingly, parents of children with autism spectrum disorders often report high levels of anxiety, depression, and everyday stress from parenting (DeMeyer, 1979). This is further exacerbated when they realize that there is no cure for autism, and services that can be of real assistance are often insufficient to meet their needs as caretakers and the needs of their child.

Implications for practice:

Based on an examination of past and current policy provisions concerning autism, a number of problems have arisen in regards to social work involvement and intervention. Due to the nature of autism only recently becoming an educational classification, social workers and other educational professionals should be trained to understand the disorder and its severity. In 1989, Munoz made the case that personnel preparation in the field of autism had been inadequate. Her admonition is no less accurate today. This is true not only of social workers, but teachers, school psychologist, residential care workers, family counselors, and other professionals could benefit from intensive pre-service and in-service training on autism. State programming policies also must be implemented fully in order that proposed interventions meet local needs and convictions (Moroz, 1989) Further, many professionals can be in the forefront of community education which also is needed to increase awareness of autism. Such efforts could generate support for the development and awareness of services in most communities. What is more, they will be helpful to families to cope with their autistic child's behaviors with understanding and without judgment.

According to Barnett (1995), early intervention with a special needs child on a pre-school level can produce large short-term benefits for children in regard to their intelligence quotient (IQ), school achievement, grade retention, placement, and social adjustment. It is important that pediatricians and other medical personnel receive the necessary training in recognizing the symptoms of autism, since they have frequent contact with the child and family.

However, few university degree programs prepare them to work with autistic children and their families.

Pharmacological management can sometimes help decrease an autistic child's behaviors to a more manageable level, information about which social workers should be familiar. The goal of medications is to reduce dysfunctional behaviors to allow the autistic individual to take advantage of educational and behavioral interventions.

Funding for training and implementation of a Lovaas style method also can significantly increase the movement of preschool age autistic children to a least restrictive environment in their school age years. It also would reduce the overall cost of special education due to decreased enrollment in a segregated setting. However, both programs have their drawbacks. The Lovaas Style intensive behavior modification program, the most statistically successful overall, can also be the most costly and demanding. The state and local Board of Education initially would have to invest more funds to provide a one-to-one student-teacher ratio to make the program most effective. Also, staff would have to provide the teaching and structure of the program to already overwhelmed families. To be successful, an approach should be flexible in nature, rely on positive reinforcement, be re-evaluated on a regular basis, and provide a smooth transition from home to school to community environments. A quality program will also incorporate training and support systems for the caregivers as well. Rarely can a family, classroom teacher or other caregiver provide effective habilitation for a person with autism unless they are offered consultation or in-service training by a specialist knowledgeable about the disability (Moroz, 1989).

Students with autism should have training in vocational skills and community living skills at the earliest possible age. Learning to cross a street safely, to make a simple purchase or to ask assistance when needed are critical skills that may be difficult, even for those with average intelligence levels. Social workers can assist in this area by becoming knowledgeable about the programs and educating families about the different type of learning programs that are out there for their child.

High Information Seeking Behavior of Parents

To cope, many parents of autistic children use a form of "high information seeking" to obtain support services for them. High information seeking also is seen as an adaptive coping response because it may influence parents to learn how to help their child effectively. High information seeking, however, also may suggest that mothers are relying solely on themselves to obtain information, rather than incorporating professional help into their support network (Rodrigue, Morgan & Geffkin, 1990). This is prevalent in the parents' "self education" about different education modalities, such as applied behavior analysis. The benefits of involving parents in their children's education are well documented and routinely practiced by school social workers. Family involvement in the education of an autistic child at school and at home becomes more critical because the child's successful development of independent living skills, and the family's ability to maintain the young person at home, hinges partially on the comprehensiveness and continuity of the child's education (Munoz, 1989).

Professional Support for Parents

Parents should be taught about the numerous professional supports that are available to them (eg. homemaker, respite and child care, and transportation). They also should be taught the importance of behavior modification and how to become more aware of the substance of their child's Individual Education Plan (IEP). This is especially important during the transition phase from preschool to school age. It is then that parents and social workers, in partnership, can begin to advocate for the best services possible, and to reduce stress level of the parent during this period. They must be allowed the option of focusing on their family needs without being blamed for their child's disability.

A supportive and educational framework has been shown to be very important in helping parents cope with their child's disability upon initial diagnosis, and to network with other families with autistic children. Zeanah (2002) reports that supports, appraisals, and family coping strategies are important areas of strength that may mediate stress in families of children with disabilities and promote adaptation (p.306). Note, too, that anxiety about one's competence in the parenting role may affect a parent's ability to implement a behavior management program successfully. This seems particularly important for mothers of autistic children because treatment programs for autistic children usually require considerable parental involvement (Rodrigue, Morgan & Geffkin, 1990).

Turbiville and Marquis (2001) found in their study that activities in which fathers could participate with their wives or partners were clearly the activities most likely to attract fathers. The preference for family-oriented activities included participation in father-child offerings such as

"Daddy and Me" and informational programs where both mothers and fathers were invited. Involving fathers in the equal sharing of caretaking responsibilities should be integral to any supportive programming advocated by social workers today. The child will reap the benefit, as will the overburdened mother. The unforeseen return will be the dividend for the father himself who will flourish as a fully engaged parent.

In conclusion, we must continue to actively support families on early intervention and preschool teams, where they collaboratively can help families coordinate the complex array of services that families encounter during this transition stage. Parents need the best information about autism possible, and they need support from professionals in order to understand and navigate this disorder. Training sessions where professionals and parents learn to collaborate is essential for the bio-psycho-social well being of the child with autism.

FOR EVERYONES LIBRARY -A LIST OF BOOKS ON AUTISM

1. <u>Ten Things Every Child with Autism Wishes You Knew</u>. Ellen Notbohm, parent and autism columnist, tries to empower parents, encourage them to trust their instincts, and find balance in their lives. An uplifting book, with practical advice on everything from meltdowns to sensory overload, from a mother who has "been there" too.

2. <u>Autism Spectrum Disorders: The Complete Guide to Understanding Autism, Asperger's Syndrome, Pervasive Developmental Disorder, and Other ASDs</u>. Long title but a very worthwhile book for parents starting their autism journey. Chantal Sicile-Kira walks you through the diagnosis, treatment options and coping strategies, from her dual perspective as a former case manager for people with disabilities and as a parent of an adult son with autism.

3. <u>Could It Be Autism?: A Parent's Guide to the First Signs and Next Steps</u>. b y Nancy Wiseman tells you

how to find out if your child is developmentally delayed as early as four months of age. The book provides checklists, discusses screening tests, and, if your child has autism, tells you how to design an effective treatment program to help him reach his potential. It says taking action is better than waiting to see if autism develops.

4. The First Year: Autism Spectrum Disorders: An Essential Guide for the Newly Diagnosed Child . A second book by First Signs' Nancy Wiseman takes parents beyond the diagnosis into health care, insurance and educational concerns.

5. Toilet Training for Individuals with Autism or Other Developmental Issues by Maria Wheeler. Children with autism and PDD can be especially hard to toilet train. This popular guide has many tips and examples of how to teach youngsters, through repetition, rewards, picture schedules and reducing sensory problems.

Diets and Biomedical Treatments

6. The Autism & ADHD Diet: A Step-by-Step Guide to Hope and Healing by Living Gluten Free and Casein Free (GFCF) and Other Interventions by Barrie Silberberg, mother of a boy with Asperger's Syndrome. Her son's behavioral symptoms improved dramatically after starting a diet free of gluten, casein, artificial dyes and preservatives.

7. The Kid-Friendly ADHD and Autism Cookbook: The Ultimate Guide to the Gluten-Free, Casein-Free Diet . A popular book by two Defeat Autism Now practitioners, developmental pediatrician Pamela Compart M.D. and nutritionist Dana Laake. Advice for feeding picky eaters, and a good explanation of how and why the diet can work. Recipes include information on calories, protein, fiber, etc., per serving. Updated edition with 100 new recipes and advice for packing school lunches.

8. No More Meltdowns: Positive Strategies for Managing and Preventing Out-Of-Control Behavior by Lisa Lewis, Ph.D. One of the first books

to explain the gluten-free, casein-free diet and how it can help treat autism. Lewis runs the Autism Network for Dietary Intervention with Karyn Seroussi (below). Her explanation of the science behind the diet is not as easy to follow as Seroussi's; but this book has more than 150 recipes for breads, cakes, candy, chili, mac and cheese, more.

9. Special Diets for Special Kids Two by Lisa Lewis Ph.D. A sequel to her first book (above) with more than 175 new gluten-free, casein-free recipes for peanut butter bread, bananaberry shake, oven fries, barbequed chicken pie and other foods that kids will eat.

10. Healing the New Childhood Epidemics: Autism, ADHD, Asthma, and Allergies: The Groundbreaking Program for the 4-A Disorders by Kenneth Bock M.D. and Cameron Stauth. They say that a child's genetics "load the gun, and environment pulls the trigger." Environmental assaults on the developing immune system may include heavy metals, viruses, vaccines and poor nutrition. Dr. Bock uses a detective approach in presenting case studies.

Broader in scope than *Children with Starving Brains,* with a focus on allergies and other conditions.

11. Unraveling the Mystery of Autism and Pervasive Developmental Disorder: A Mother's Story of Research and Recovery by Karyn Seroussi. An excellent book for parents considering a gluten-free, casein-free diet to treat autism or PDD. Seroussi's son recovered from autism by strictly adhering to this diet. She provides a thorough discussion of her son's problems with foods, intestinal yeast, and vaccines.

12. Enzymes for Autism and other Neurological Conditions. Author/parent Karen L. DeFelice discusses the role of enzymes in helping people with autism digest foods that create problems for them. Many parents use enzymes in addition to a gluten-free, milk-free diet, while some use them instead of the diet.

13. Children with Starving Brains: A Medical Treatment Guide for Autism Spectrum Disorder by Jacquelyn

McCandless M.D. Outlines treatments based on the theory that autism is a biomedical illness resulting in brain malnutrition. Genetics, in combination with exposure to pesticides and heavy metals in vaccines, can lead to immune system problems, gut dysfunction, and yeast and viral infections, says Dr. McCandless, whose granddaughter has autism.

14. Changing the Course of Autism: A Scientific Approach for Parents and Physicians by Bryan Jepson M.D. with Jane Johnson. Discusses immune system and detoxification problems in autism, brain inflammation, the effect of mercury, and autism as an environmental illness. Dr. Jepson is medical director of Thoughtful House, an autism research and treatment center in Texas. "*Changing the Course of Autism* was written with physicians in mind. It contains over 50 pages of references to published scientific studies supporting the information and treatment options provided by Dr. Jepson," said Unlocking Autism, which asked parents to buy the book for their pediatricians.

15. Special Diets for Special People: Understanding and

Implementing a Gluten-Free and Casein-Free Diet to Aid in the Treatment of Autism and Related Developmental Disorders. The newest how-to book, with more than 150 recipes, by GFCF diet guru Lisa Lewis, Ph.D.

16. Healing and Preventing Autism: A Complete Guide. . Comedienne Jenny McCarthy, whose son recovered from autism, interviews Jerry Kartzinel M.D. about Defeat Autism Now biomedical treatments. Dr. Kartzinel simplifies biomed theories and discusses steps parents can take while waiting to see a DAN doctor. He provides dosages for supplements, explains yeast overgrowth and diets, and outlines lab tests. Aimed at parents new to biomed. People seeking more details may prefer the Bock and McCandless books (above).

Overviews of Autism, PDD and Asperger's Syndrome

17. 1001 Great Ideas for Teaching and Raising Children with Autism Spectrum Disorders. by Ellen Notbohm

and Veronica Zysk. Practical tips and strategies for helping a child with his learning problems, sensory integration, communication, behavior and social skills. Books by Notbohm are a pleasure to read.

18. The Complete Guide to Asperger's Syndrome, by Dr. Tony Attwood. One of the best books on AS, Attwood relies on research and personal accounts of people with Asperger's to present a positive, enlightening picture. Includes information on sensory and coordination problems, and difficulties with empathy in people with Asperger's.

19. Parent Survival Manual: A Guide to Crisis Resolution in Autism and Related Developmental Disorders, edited by Eric Schopler, Ph.D., founder, Division TEACCH at University of North Carolina. The TEACCH method is used in many schools. Based on interviews with parents and behavioral experts, this book provides solutions to common problems involving aggression, communication, hygiene, social skills, eating, and sleep.

20. Overcoming Autism: Finding the Answers, Strategies, and Hope That Can Transform a Child's

Life by Lynn Koegel Ph.D. (who was featured on *The Supernanny*) and Claire LaZebnik. Teaches how to use behavior modification, from both a clinician's and a parent's perspective. Koegel uses a form of behavior treatment called Pivotal Response Treatment (PRT). PRT targets certain *pivotal* skills, such as motivation, that affect development in many other areas.

21. The Way I See It: A Personal Look at Autism and Asperger's . Temple Grandin, the subject of a new HBO movie, discusses her intriguing life with autism. Born at a time when autism was not widely understood, Grandin overcame many obstacles to become a professor and advocate. She believes autism gives her special insight into the animal world, contributing to her noteworthy career in animal science. Her book offers practical advice for understanding autism, from an insider's perspective.

22. The OASIS Guide to Asperger Syndrome: Completely Revised and Updated: Advice, Support, Insight, and Inspiration by Patricia Bashe and

Barbara Kirby, the founder of the popular Asperger web site, OASIS.

Applied Behavior Analysis (ABA) and Verbal Behavior (VB)

23. <u>Let Me Hear Your Voice: A Family's Triumph Over Autism</u> by Catherine Maurice. Maurice writes a personal and emotional account about discovering that two of her children had autism and how both children recovered through ABA therapy. Though the experience of recovery is not universal, her book is a powerful testimony to the benefits of Applied Behavior Analysis.

24. <u>Behavioral Intervention for Young Children With Autism: A Manual for Parents and Professionals</u>, edited by Catherine Maurice, Gina Green and Stephen C. Luce. An excellent how-to manual for families starting a home teaching program using Applied Behavior Analysis. Includes a chapter on how to pay for ABA, which can be costly, and samples of data collection sheets and programs.

25. <u>Right from the Start: Behavioral Intervention for Young Children with Autism</u> by Sandra L. Harris and Mary Jane Weiss, ABA experts at Rutgers. A guide to Applied Behavioral Analysis methods and how they can be used to teach speech, language, social skills and self-help skills through repetition and rewards. Harris and Weiss help parents evaluate school programs, home ABA and center-based ABA.

26. <u>The Verbal Behavior Approach: How to Teach Children With Autism and Related Disorders</u> by Mary Lynch Barbera, a Board Certified Behavior Analyst and parent of a child with autism, and Tracy Rasmussen. One of the few parent-oriented books about using Verbal Behavior to teach communication, speech, self-help skills, potty-training and more.

27. <u>A Work in Progress: Behavior Management Strategies and A Curriculum for Intensive Behavioral Treatment of Autism</u> edited by Drs. Ron Leaf and John McEachin. This ABA classic provides practical advice and easy-to-understand explanations about how to set up an ABA program. It discusses how to teach toilet training, social skills, play skills and conversation, along with how to address eating

problems and disruptive behavior.

28. <u>Educate Toward Recovery: Turning the Tables on Autism</u> by Robert Schramm, a Board Certified Behavior Analyst. A teaching manual for parents who are new to the concepts and language of Verbal Behavior therapy. He includes information on children who don't respond to conventional ABA methods, and on how VB can be used along with the Relationship Development Intervention method.

Getting What Your Child Needs From the School District

29. <u>Wrightslaw: From Emotions to Advocacy: The Special Education Survival Guide</u> . A must-read for every parent trying to get the best program possible from the school system. Lawyer Peter Wright and psychotherapist Pamela Wright explain special education law, how to interpret and and use test scores, how to write letters to school officials, and how to be an effective advocate. Easy to understand. Includes sample letters for you to use.

30. Educating Children with Autism by the National Research Council. An excellent resource for parents seeking research to support their educational requests. It examines the research and claims behind the major teaching methods; identifies the characteristics of effective preschool and school programs; and discusses ways to better prepare teachers and parents.

31. Wrightslaw: All About IEPs , the newest book by Peter and Pamela Wright, uses a question-and-answer format to explain IEPS, ESY and other confusing jargon to parents who are new to special education. Also a handy reference guide for experienced advocates who need to look up answers quickly at meetings.

Speech Therapy

32. Baby Babble - Speech-Enhancing DVD for Babies and Toddlers . Created by speech pathologists, this popular DVD uses sign language, facial exercises, and speech sounds and words to promote speech

development in babies, late talkers and kids with developmental delays. Volume 2 is Baby Babble 2 - First Words: P B M sounds.

33. Do-Watch-Listen-Say: Social and Communication Intervention for Children with Autism. Kathleen Ann Quill show parents, teachers and speech pathologists how to teach children social and communication skills. Easy-to-read. Includes a tool for assessing a child's language.

34. Videos by Bee Smart Baby Vocabulary Builder 1 introduce words through simple scenes that show different types of the object being taught. Good for children with speech delays, PDD or autism.

35. Baby Signing Time Volume 1 DVD teaches signs and words to toddlers and preschoolers. Engaging format.

Therapies and Teaching Methods

36. Engaging Autism: Using the Floortime Approach to Help Children Relate, Communicate, and Think .

Stanley Greenspan M.D. and Serena Wieder Ph.D. explain the Floortime method of playing with a young child in order to teach social interaction and communication skills. They encourage a broader view of autism than traditionally used.

37. You're Going to Love This Kid: Teaching Students With Autism in the Inclusive Classroom by inclusion expert Paula Kluth Ph.D. A guide to understanding students with autism and teaching them effectively in a "regular" classroom. Ideas for improving reading, handling behavior and promoting friendships with non-disabled children. A great gift for your child's teachers. Kluth's newest book, Just Give Him The Whale!, shows how to use a student's special interests to teach academics, social skills and communication.

38. Relationship Development Intervention with Young Children: Social and Emotional Development Activities for Asperger Syndrome, Autism, PDD and NLD by Steven E. Gutstein. Dr. Gutstein developed the Relationship Development Intervention Program (RDI) to help children become excited about

expanding their world, rather than to be afraid of it. Many families are using RDI in addition to ABA and other teaching methods.

39. Ten Things Your Student with Autism Wishes You Knew by popular author Ellen Notbohm. "Chapter One, 'Learning is Circular,' all the way through chapter ten, 'Teach Me How to Fish,' fills those of us who love someone with autism with hope and encouragement. We can do this," says Nancy Cale of Unlocking Autism.

Other Books on Autism:

40. ***Children with Autism: A Parent's Guide*** by Michael D. Powers, ed. (Woodbine House, 1989). Part of the series *The Special Needs Collection*. Replaced by second edition. Guide to treatments, education and legal problems. Includes glossary, reading list, and lengthy resource guide of national and local organizations in USA. Foreword by Beverly Sills, Introduction by Bernard Rimland. Chapters: "What is autism?", "Adjusting to your child's diagnosis", "Medical problems, treatments, and professionals", "Daily life with your child", "Children with autism

and their families", "Your child's development", "Finding the right educational program", "Legal rights and hurdles", "Becoming an advocate", "The years ahead: adults with autism".http://www.woodbinehouse.com/CWA.html ISBN: 0933149166 (paperback, 368 pages). *[autism,parent,intro]*

41. ***Asperger's Syndrome: A Guide for Parents and Professionals*** by Anthony Attwood. (London: Jessica Kingsley Publishers, 1998). Forward by Lorna Wing. Reader: clear, sympathetic and full of understanding. http://www.jkp.com/catalogue/autism/att_asp.html ISBN: 1853025771 (paperback, 176 pages).*[autism,aspergers,parent,intro]*

42. ***Autism: Handle with Care! Understanding and Managing Behavior of Children and Adults with Autism*** by Gail Gillingham. (Future Education a.k.a. Future Horizons, 1995). Details many anecdotes from real life situations which clarify exactly why an autistic person reacts bizarrely to normal stimuli the rest of us would find unremarkable. Author writes from an empathetic perspective. One reader:

excellent book explaining sensory difficulties experienced by people with autism. ISBN: 1885477147 (paperback). *[autism,intro]*

43. ***A Parent's Guide to Autism: Answers to the Most Common Questions*** by Charles A. Hart. (Pocket Book Publishers, 1993). Called excellent by AUTISM list member. Structured so that you can understand parts of it without tackling the whole book. Includes list of books and resources. ISBN: 0671750992 (paperback, 244 pages). *[autism,intro,parent]*

44. ***The World of the Autistic Child: Understanding and Treating Autistic Spectrum Disorders*** by Bryna Siegel. (New York: Oxford University Press, 1996). Discusses diagnostic process and gives descriptions of the differences between Autism/PDD/Aspergers/Retts Syndrome etc. Author worked at the PDD clinic at the Langley Porter Psychiatric Institute at the University of California. Parent: couldn't put it down. http://www.oup-usa.org/docs/0195076672.html ISBN: 0195076672

(hardcover, 351 pages); ISBN: 0195119177 (paperback, 368 pages, 1998).
[autism,se,treatment,aspergers,pdd,intro]

45. ***The Biology of the Autistic Syndromes, 2nd edition*** by Christopher Gillberg & Mary Coleman. (Cambridge University Press, 1992). Part of the series *Clinics in Developmental Medicine*. Number 126 in series. Also Praeger/Greenwood Publishing Group, Westport, CT. Among other things, a good source of information on specific & related syndromes. Includes chapter of population studies on how prevalent autism is. Also it has a section recommending tests that should be run during an autism workup. Also London: Mac Keith. ISBN: 0521432286 (hardcover, 317 pages). *[autism,text]*

46. ***Autism and Asperger's Syndrome*** by Uta Frith, ed. (Cambridge: Cambridge University Press, 1991). Also New York. Reprinted 1994. 247 pages. Reader: a good book on Asperger Syndrome. Includes chapter: The autobiographical writings of three Asperger syndrome adults" by Happe. ISBN:

052138608X (paperback); ISBN: 0521384486 (hardcover). *[autism,aspergers]*

47. ***Autism: Explaining the Enigma*** by Uta Frith. (Oxford: Basil Blackwell, 1989). Recommended by some AUTISM-list participants as a good introduction to autism. See also 2003 2nd edition. http://www.blackwellpublishers.co.uk/scripts/webbooke.idc?ISBN=0631168249 ISBN: 0631168249 (paperback, 204 pages, Cambridge, MA, 1991). *[autism,intro]*

48. ***The Ultimate Stranger; the autistic child*** by Carl H. Delacato. (Garden City, N.Y.: Doubleday, 1974). Delacato's thesis is that autism is neuro-genic and not psycho-genic in origin. Deals almost entirely with sensory problems affecting autistic children. Topics include sensory hypersensitivity, hyposensitivity, and "white noise", by which it refers to a kind of internal interference. ISBN: 0385010745 (paperback, 225 pages); ISBN: 0878794468 (Arena; Academic Therapy Publications, paperback, 226 pages). *[autism,intro]*

49. ***Handbook of autism and Pervasive Developmental Disorders*** by Donald J. Cohen & Anne M. Donnellan, ed. (New York: John Wiley & Sons, 1987). Includes fairly extensive bibliographies. See 2nd and 3rd editions. ISBN: 0471812315 (Silver Springs, MD: Winston, 757 pages). *[autism,intro,text]*

50. ***Infantile Autism: The Syndrome and Its Implications for a Neural Theory of Behavior*** by Bernard Rimland. (New York: Appleton-Century-Crofts, 1964). 282 pages. An older book that had far-reaching impact, influencing the choices being made as to the method of treatment. Photo-reproduced reprint is available. ISBN: 0829000615 ; ISBN: 0134643135 . *[autism]*

51. ***Handbook of Autism and Pervasive Developmental Disorders, 2nd edition*** by Donald J. Cohen, editor & Fred R. Volkmar, editor. (John Wiley & Sons, 1997). Textbook. http://info.med.yale.edu/chldstdy/autism/page19.html See 3rd edition. ISBN: 0471532428 (hardcover, 1092 pages).*[autism,intro,text]*

52. ***Behavioral Intervention for Young Children with Autism: A manual for parents and professionals*** by Catherine Maurice, editor, Gina Green, editor & Stephen Luce, editor. (Austin: Pro-Ed, 1996). 24 contributors. Primary compiler is Catherine Maurice, who wrote the very popular account, *Let Me Hear Your Voice*. http://www.proedinc.com/store/7816.html ISBN: 0890796831 (paperback, 400 pages). *[autism,behavioral,treatment]*

53. ***Clinical Assessment Options for Children with Autism and Related Disorders*** by Sidney M. Baker & Jon Pangborn, editor. (1996). 40 pages. Protocol for medical practitioners compiled from 1995 Dallas medical conference, "Defeat Autism Now!". Outlines biomedical tests, conclusions to be drawn, and followup. This procedure and booklet is often refered to as the *DAN Protocol*, and I've also seen the title listed as *DEFEAT AUTISM NOW! Clinical Options Manual for Physicians*. http://www.autism.com/ari/dan.html *[autism,treatment]*

54. ***Teaching Developmentally Disabled Children: The Me Book*** by Ole Ivar Lovaas. (Austin, Texas: Pro-Ed, 1981). Available from publisher at 8700 Shoal Creek Blvd, Austin, Texas 78757, 1-512-451-3246. Describes a home-based program for behavior modification therapy. This book is highly recommended by practitioners of the Lovaas method. As of 5/96, I heard that a revision is in the works. http://www.proedinc.com/store/1213.html ISBN: 0936104783 (paperback, 250 pages, University Park Press, 1981). *[autism,treatment,behavioral]*

55. ***Biological Treatments for Autism and PDD*** by William Shaw, Bernard Rimland, Pamela Scott, Karyn Seroussi, Lisa Lewis & Bruce Semon. (Sunflower Press, 1997). I think its working title was once *The Biological Basis of Autism and PDD*. Covers yeast, gluten/casein, and vitamin treatments. Initially not in many bookstores; call 913-341-6207. http://www.greatplainslaboratory.com/page37.htm ISBN: 0966123808 (paperback, 303 pages).*[autism,disability,allergy,pdd,treatment]*

56. ***Special Diets for Special Kids*** by Lisa Lewis. (Arlington, Texas: Future Horizons, 1998). http://www.futurehorizons-autism.com/page.htmlhttp://www.futurehorizons-autism.com/book2.html Also Jessica Kingsley, 1999, 252 pages. http://www.jkp.com/catalogue/autism/lew_spe.html ISBN: 1885477449 (paperback, 252 pages). *[nutrition,allergy,treatment]*

57. ***Unlocking the Potential of Secretin*** by Victoria Beck & Gary Beck. As of October 1998, booklet due out later in the month from Autism Research International. http://www.autism.com/ari/secretin.html *[autism,treatment]*

58. ***Sensory Integration and the Child*** by Jean Ayres. (Los Angeles, California: Western Psychological Services, 1979). Also 1983. With Jeff Robbins. Reader: easy to understand information on the sensory system. ISBN: 0874241588 . *[autism,si,treatment]*

59. ***Autism Treatment Guide*** by Elizabeth K. Gerlach. (Portland, Oregon: Four Leaf Press, 1993). 130 pages. $7. Handbook containing brief descriptions of autism treatments and resources. Also considered a pretty good introduction to Autism, e.g. for Parents. Won Elizabeth the 1994 "Outstanding Parent Achievement Award". See Third Edition of 2003. *[autism,treatment,intro]*

60. ***Dietary Intervention as a Therapy in the Treatment of Autism and PDD*** by Beth Crowell & Andy Crowell. (Housatonic, Mass.: 1992). Private publication. Includes references for follow-up reading. Reader: The first half of the book is great-- lots of references to do follow up reading for those so inclined. Excellent chocolate chip cookie recipe. *[autism,pdd]*

61. ***Let Me Hear Your Voice: A Family's Triumph over Autism*** by Catherine Maurice. (New York: Fawcett Columbia, 1993). Also Knopf. Mother's account of using the Lovaas's Behavior Modification method with her children. Also has comments on Holding

Therapy. Includes a good description of the grieving process parents go through. This has also been highly recommended as a good book for a parent who is depressed over having an autistic child.ISBN: 0679408630 (hardcover, 371 pages, Knopf, 1993); ISBN: 0449906647 (paperback, 371 pages, 1994).
[autism,account,behavioral,holding,treatment]

62. ***Thinking in Pictures: and Other Reports of my Life with Autism*** by Temple Grandin. (New York: Bantam, 1995). Not really an account of Temple's life so much as her explanation of autism, particularly her own, citing examples from her own life and others she has talked to and read. It also discusses education and treatment. One reader calls it terrific: better than *Emergence*.... http://www.autism.org/temple/ http://www.grandin.com/inc/book.html ISBN: 0385477929 (hardcover, 222 pages, Doubleday, 1995); ISBN: 0679772898 (paperback, 222 pages, Vintage edition, 1996); ISBN: 0307275655 (paperback, 304 pages, Vintage, 2006, ISBN-13: 978-0307275653). *[autism,account]*

63. ***Nobody Nowhere: The Extraordinary Autobiography of an Autistic*** by Donna Williams. (Random, 1992). Doubleday, 1992. 219 pages. Also Corgi Books. The autobiography of an autistic woman; bestseller in early 1993. Shows an autistic person surviving an abusive family situation; painful to read. List member reactions: some describe it as truly amazing and very valuable; others don't recommend it at all. http://www.jkp.com/catalogue/autism/wil_nob.html ISBN: 0385254253 ; ISBN: 0552995126 (paperback, Corgi, 1993); ISBN: 0380722178 (paperback, 248 pages, Avon Books, 1994); ISBN: 0812920422 (hardcover, 219 pages, New York: Time Books, 1992, LCCN: 92-053669); ISBN: 1853027189 (Jessica Kingsley, 1998); ISBN: 0944993818 (audio cassette, abridged, Audio Literature, 1994). *[autism, account]*

64. ***Emergence: Labeled Autistic*** by Temple Grandin & Margaret M. Scariano. (Navato, California: Arena Press, 1986). Since updated in 1991. This is an autobiographical book by Temple Grandin, with

Margaret Scariano. It offers insight into the frustrations that people labeled autistic have during the time they are trying to develop an ability to communicate. This is considered a rare autobiographical account in as much as the majority of the people with autism have not developed such sophisticated communication abilities. Very highly recommended by a number of readers. ISBN: 0878795243 (paperback, 183 pages);ISBN: 0710400632 (Costello, 1986). *[autism,account]*

65. ***Somebody Somewhere: Breaking Free from the World of Autism*** by Donna Williams. (1993). Also Doubleday, 1994. Donna explores the four years since her diagnosis and her attempts to leave her 'world under glass' and live normally. Shows some of the distortions of perception an autistic person may have, and possibilities for un-learning them. But hard to read without having 1st read the other book, as it refers to events in that book.http://www.jkp.com/catalogue/autism/wil_nob.html ISBN: 0812925246 (paperback, Times Books, 1995); ISBN: 0812922875 (hardcover, 238 pages, New York: Time Books, 1994); ISBN: 0385255004

(paperback, Bantam Books of Canada); ISBN: 1853027197 (paperback, 208 pages, Jessica Kingsley, 1998, 1995); ISBN: 0552141984 (paperback, 288 pages, Corgi, 1995); ISBN: 0944993869 (audio cassette, abridged, Audio Literature, 1994). *[autism, account]*

66. ***There's a Boy in Here*** by Judy Barron & Sean Barron. (Chapmans, 1993). Sean Barron and his mother, Judy Barron report on their experiences with autism. Sean has autism. His is one of very few autobiographical accounts. And it gives unusual, exceptionally clear insights into the disability and its many manifestations. There is much in this book that supports what has been seen through facilitated communication. ISBN: 1885477864 (paperback, 279 pages, Future Horizons, 2002); ISBN: 0671761110 (264 pages, New York: Simon & Schuster, 1992); ISBN: 0380722925 (paperback, Avon Books, 1992, reprint). *[autism, account]*

67. ***Son-Rise*** by Barry Neil Kaufman. (New York: Harper & Row, 1976). A father's account. About Raun Kahlil Kaufman. No longer in print. ISBN:

0060122765 (hardcover, 153 pages); ISBN: 0446921106 (paperback, Warner, 1979); ISBN: 0446893471 (paperback, 221 pages, Warner, 1997). *[autism,account]*

68. ***The Sound of a Miracle, A Child's Triumph Over Autism*** by Annabel Stehli. (New York: Doubleday, 1991). Account of author's daughter Georgiana's astonishing recovery from autism after receiving Auditory Integration Training from Dr. Guy Berard, a physician in Annecy, France. Note the book is out in a second edition (below). http://www.vision3d.com/adhd/autism.shtml ISBN: 0380717395 ; ISBN: 0385411405 (4th Estate, 1992, paperback).*[autism,account,ait]*

69. ***Mixed Blessings*** by William Christopher & Barbara Christopher. (Nashville: Abingdon Press, 1989). 224 pages. TV's Father Mulcahy of M*A*S*H and his real-life family share the story of raising son, Ned, who has autism. The Christophers used the intensive and controversial Doman-Delacato techniques to educate and treat Ned at home. The book has a moving section on Ned's troubled adolescence, when he developed epilepsy and violent rages, and the

family's search for a group residence that would fit Ned's needs. ISBN: 0380709996 ; ISBN: 0687270847 . *[autism,account]*

70. ***Son-Rise: The Miracle Continues*** by Barry Neil Kaufman & Samarhia Lyte Kaufman. (Kramer, 1994?). Update of *Son-Rise* including introduction by their once-autistic son. Also covers five other families who have used the Son-Rise program for their special children. ISBN: 0915811537 (hardcover, 347 pages); ISBN: 0915811618 (paperback, 347 pages). *[autism,account]*

71. ***Without Reason: A family copes with Two Generations of Autism*** by Charles A. Hart. (New York: Harper & Row, 1989). Written by a man who had an autistic brother and (in the '70s) an autistic son. Reader: inspiring, readable, intelligent. Reader: good account to be read by teen siblings because it describes a sibling's experience. ISBN: 0451169409 ; ISBN: 0060161434 (292 pages); ISBN: 1885477694 (292 pages, Future Horizons).*[autism,account,family]*

72. ***An Anthropologist on Mars*** by Oliver Sacks. (1995). Book describing several people with neurological anomalies including autistic people. Includes some art by autistic artist. ISBN: 0679756973 (paperback, Vintage Books, 1996); ISBN: 0679439560 (audio cassette, Random House, 1995).*[autism,account,disability]*

73. ***The Siege*** by Clara Claiborne Park. (Little & Brown, 1967). The first eight years of an autistic child, a mother's account. See edition with epilogue, below.ISBN: 1112233245 (New York: Harcourt, Brace & World 1967, 279 pages); ISBN: 0316690767 ; ISBN: 090067511X . *[autism,account]*

74. ***Soon Will Come The Light: A View From Inside the Autism Puzzle*** by Thomas A. McKean. (Arlington, Texas: Future Education a.k.a. Future Horizons, 1994). Thomas McKean has autism and is a contributor to the AUTISM e-mail mailing list. AUTISM mailing list reader: he explains a lot of stuff we question every day on this list. ISBN:

9994393324 (paperback); ISBN: 1885477112 (paperback, 155 pages). *[autism,account]*

75. ***Like Color to the Blind: Soul Searching and Soul Finding*** by Donna Williams. (New York: Times Books, 1996). Canada: Doubleday. Third in series.http://www.jkp.com/catalogue/autism/wil_nob.html ISBN: 0385255950 (paperback, Doubleday, 1996); ISBN: 0812926404 (paperback, 288 pages);ISBN: 1853027200 (Jessica Kingsley, 1998). *[autism,account]*

76. ***News From The Border: A Mother's Memoir of Her Autistic Son*** by Jane Taylor McDonnell & Paul McDonnell. (New York: Ticknor & Fields, 1993). 376 pages. About Paul McDonnell, a high-functioning autistic person, who wrote an afterword. Reader: intelligent and sensitive account. Note: 0939394040 is an invalid ISBN that was used by Amazon for the book. I no longer find reference to that number, but believe the book had a 1993 and a 1997 edition, but cannot find a second valid ISBN. ISBN: 0395605741 (hardcover, 376

pages); ISBN: 0939394040 (paperback, Jane McDonnell 1997). *[autism,account]*

77. ***Fighting for Tony*** by Mary Callahan. (New York: Simon & Schuster, 1987). Describes mother's experience dealing with her son's cerebral allergies & the son's dramatic improved after cow's milk was eliminated from his diet. ISBN: 0671632655 (172 pages); ISBN: 0671644564 . *[autism,account,allergy]*

78. ***Laughing and Loving with Autism: A Collection of 'Real Life' Warm & Humorous Stories*** by R. Wayne Gilpin, ed. (Future Horizons, 1993). 126 pages. Short vignettes about persons with autism. ISBN: 188547704X (paperback). *[autism,account]*

79. ***Paid for the Privilege: Hearing the Voices of Autism*** by Dan Reed. (Madison, Wisconsin: DRI Press, 1996). 162 pages. *[autism,account,fc]*

80. ***Dancing in the Rain: Stories of Exceptional Progress by Parents of Children with Special Needs*** by Annabel Stehli, ed. (Georgiana, 1995).

Followup to *The Sound of a Miracle*: stories about families experiences with AIT. Not all the stories concern autism. Also tells what it is like to have super-sensitive hearing. ISBN: 0964483807 (paperback). *[autism,account,ait]*

81. ***When Snow Turns to Rain: One Family's Struggle to Solve the Riddle of Autism*** by Craig B. Schulze. (Rockville, Md.: Woodbine House, 1993). About Craig's son Jordan Schulze. Includes accounts of the Options method and the Higashi school. Jordan had late-onset autism and is one of the children described in Robert Catalano's book *When Autism Strikes: Families Cope With Childhood Disintegrative Disorder*.http://www.woodbinehouse.com/str.html ISBN: 0933149638 (paperback, 216 pages). *[autism,account]*

82. *A miracle to believe in* by Barry Neil Kaufman. (Garden City, N.Y.: Doubleday, 1981). The entire book is online. http://www.option.org/miracle/index.htmlISBN: 0449201082 (Fawcett Crest/Ballantine, 313 pages). *[autism,account]*

83. ***A Slant of Sun: One Child's Courage*** by Beth Kephart. (W.W. Norton, 1998). Account of the author's son, Jeremy, who was diagnosed PDD-NOS. Finalist for 1998 National Book Award in nonfiction category; chosen as one of the best books of 1998 by both Salon Magazine and the Philadelphia Inquirer; and won the author a 1998 Leeway Grant for Nonfiction. http://www.pov3.com/slant.html ISBN: 0393027422 (hardcover, 256 pages); ISBN: 0688172288 (paperback, 256 pages, Quill, 1999); ISBN: 1574901931 (hardcover, large print, Thomas T. Beeler). *[autism,account,pdd]*

Education Based:

84. ***Teach Me Language: A language manual for children with autism, Asperger's syndrome and related developmental disorders*** by Sabrina K. Freeman, Lorelei Dake & Isaac Tamir, illustrator. (Langley, BC, Canada: SKF Books, 1996). Book for parents and therapists to serve as the next step after *The Me Book*. Includes material on how to teach

social skills & functional language. Publisher also sells companion worksheets. One parent: highly recommended, especially if your child can read. http://fox.nstn.ca/~zacktam/ ISBN: 0965756505 (hardcover, 420 pages, 2nd edition, 1997); ISBN 0968098509 . *[autism,aspergers,behavioral,treatment,social,se]*

85. ***The Social Story Book*** by Carol Gray. (1994). 440 pages, 200 stories. I've also seen it as *The Original Social Story Book* and *Original Social Stories* or just *Social Stories*. ISBN: 1885477198 . *[autism,social,se]*

86. ***The New Social Story Book*** by Carol Gray. (Future Horizons, 1994). 280p. I've also seen it as *Social Stories...all new stories teaching social skills.* and*The New Social Stories*. ISBN: 1885477201 (paperback). *[autism,se,social]*

87. ***Teaching Children with Autism: Strategies to Enhance Communication and Socialization*** by Kathleen Ann Quill, ed. (New York: Delmar, 1995).

Recommended by at least one participant of the AUTISM list as a good introduction to Autism. Includes chapters from 14 contributors including Temple Grandin, Carol Grey, Barry Prizant, Diane Twachtman, and Kathleen Quill. Another participant: "found helpful in training teachers". Includes information on modelling. http://www.delmar.com/catalog/education/ece/quill.html ISBN: 0827362692 (paperback, 315 pages). *[autism,se]*

88. *Teaching Children with Autism: Strategies for initiating positive interactions and improving learning opportunities* by Robert L. Koegel, ed & Lynn Kern Koegel, ed. (Baltimore: Paul H. Brookes, 1995). http://education.ucsb.edu/~doniel/recentbooks.html http://www.pbrookes.com/e-catalog/books/koegel-1804/index.htm ISBN: 1557661804 (paperback, 256 pages). *[autism,se]*

89. *Movement Differences and Diversity in Autism/Mental Retardation: Appreciating and Accommodating People with Communication Challenges* by Anne M. Donnellan & Martha R.

Leary. (Madison, Wisconsin: DRI Press, 1995). ISBN: 1886928002 . *[autism,fc,mr]*

90. ***Creating a Win-Win IEP for Students with Autism! A How-To Manual for Parents and Educators*** by Beth Fouse. (Future Horizons, 1996). Reader: very comprehensive IEP help guide. ISBN: 1885477287 (paperback, 172 pages, 1996); ISBN: 188547752X (hardcover, 1999).*[autism,se,parent]*

91. ***Joey and Sam: A Heartwarming Storybook About Autism, a Family, and a Brother's Love*** by Illana Katz & Edward Ritvo. (Los Angeles, California: Real Life Storybooks, 1993). Ages 4-8. A beautifully illustrated storybook for children. It focuses on a family with two sons, one of which suffers from autism. The book addresses their similarities and differences, as it follows them through daily interactions with each other, parents, and friends. Suggested for K-3.http://www.reallifestories.com/booksa.html ISBN: 1882388003 (hardcover); ISBN: 1882388062 (paperback). *[autism,fiction,children]*

92. ***Little Rainman*** by Karen L. Simmons. (Future Education, 1996). I also saw the author listed as Karen Sicoli. When someone asked online for a good book for 5 year olds, several readers recommended this book. http://www.futurehorizons-autism.com/rainman.html ISBN: 1885477295 (paperback).*[autism,children]*

93. ***The OASIS Guide to Asperger Syndrome: Advice, Support, Insights, and Inspiration*** by Patricia Romanowski Bashe & Barbara L. Kirby. (Crown Pub, 2001). See newer edition. ISBN: 0609608118 (hardcover, 467 pages). *[autism,aspergers]*

94. ***Reweaving the Autistic Tapestry - Autism, Asperger's Syndrome and ADHD*** by Lisa Blakemore-Brown. (Jessica Kingsley Publishers, 2001). ISBN: 1853027480 (paperback, 384 pages). *[autism,aspergers,adhd]*

95. ***Autism*** by Michele Engel Edwards. (Lucent Books, 2001). Part of the series *Diseases and Disorders*

Series. ISBN: 1560068299 (hardcover, 112 pages). *[autism,children]*

96. ***Art Therapy With Children on the Autistic Spectrum: Beyond Words*** by Kathy Evans & Janek Dubowski. (Jessica Kingsley Pub, 2001). ISBN: 1853028258 (paperback, 176 pages). *[autism,treatment]*

97. ***Bright Splinters of the Mind: A Personal Story of Research with Autistic Savant*** by Beate Hermelin. (Jessica Kingsley Pub, 2001). ISBN: 1853029319 (hardcover, 176 pages); ISBN: 1853029327 (paperback, 176 pages). *[autism,account]*

98. ***Autism*** by Elaine Landau. (Franklin Watts, 2001). The author has written a number of non-fiction books including books explaining illnesses, aimed at children, ages 9-12. ISBN: 0531117804 (hardcover, 128 pages). *[autism,children]*

99. ***Understanding and Working With the Spectrum of Autism: An Insider's View*** by Wendy Lawson. (London: Jessica Kingsley Pub, 2001). The author was diagnosed to have an autism-spectrum disorder

after she became an adult. She also wrote her own account in *Life Behind Glass*. ISBN: 1853029718 (paperback, 276 pages). *[autism,treatment]*

100. ***Incorporating Social Goals in the Classrooms: A Guide for Teachers and Parents with High Functioning Autism and Asperger Syndrome*** by Rebecca A. Moyes. (Jessica Kingsley Pub, 2001). ISBN: 185302967X (paperback, 176 pages). *[autism,aspergers,se,parent]*

101. ***The Research Basis for Autism Intervention*** by Eric Schopler, editor, Nurit Yimiya, editor, Cory Shulman, editor & Lee M. Marcus, editor. (Plenum Pub Corp, 2001). ISBN: 030646585X (hardcover, 241 pages). *[autism,treatment]*

102. ***Autistic Thinking--This Is the Title*** by Peter Vermeulen. (Taylor & Francis Group, 2001). ISBN: 1853029955 (paperback). *[autism,account,se]*

103. ***Asperger Syndrome in the Family: Redefining Normal*** by Liane Holliday Willey. (London: Jessica Kingsley Pub, 2001). Amazon lists publisher as

'Taylor & Francis' ISBN: 1853028738 (paperback, 172 pages). *[autism,aspergers,account]*

104.***Our Journey Through High Functioning Autism and Asperger Syndrome: A Roadmap*** by Linda Andron, editor. (Jessica Kingsley Pub, 2001). Forewords by Tony Attwood and Liane Holliday Willey. ISBN: 1853029475 (paperback, 160 pages). *[autism,aspergers,account]*

105.***Diet Intervention and Autism: Implementing the Gluten Free and Casein Free Diet for Autistic Children and Adults: A Practical Guide for Parents*** by Marilyn Le Breton & Rosemary Kessick. (Jessica Kingsley Publishers, 2001). ISBN: 1853029351 (paperback, 176 pages). *[autism,nutrition,allergy]*

106.***Keys to Parenting the Child with Autism, 2nd ed*** by Marlene Targ Brill. (Hauppauge, New York: Barron's, 2001). Part of the series *Parenting Keys*. See first edition. ISBN: 0764112929 (hardcover, 200 pages). *[autism,parent]*

107. ***Breaking Autism's Barriers: A Father's Story*** by Bill Davis & Wendy Goldband Schunick. (Jessica Kingsley, 2001). ISBN: 1853029793 (paperback, 400 pages). *[autism,account]*

108. ***Autism/Asperger's: Solving the Relationship Puzzle*** by Steven Gutstein. (Future Horizons, 2001). ISBN: 1885477708 (paperback, 200 pages). *[autism,aspergers]*

109. ***Blue Bottle Mystery: An Asperger Adventure*** by Kathy Hoopmann. (Jessica Kingsley Pub, 2001). For ages 9-12. Fantasy story about a boy with Asperger Syndrome. ISBN: 1853029785 (paperback, 96 pages). *[autism,aspergers,fiction,children]*

110. ***Autism, Art, and Children: The Stories We Draw*** by Julia Kellman. (Bergin & Garvey, 2001). ISBN: 0897897358 (hardcover, 160 pages). *[autism,treatment]*

111. ***Autism and Post-Traumatic Stress Disorder: Ending Autistic Fixation*** by Ken Lenchitz. (Charles C Thomas Pub, 2001). ISBN: 0398070962

(hardcover); ISBN: 0398070970 (paperback). *[autism,treatment,psychoanalysis]*

112. ***Educating Children With Autism*** by National Research Council, editor, Catherine Lord, editor & James McGee, editor. (National Academy Press, 2001). ISBN: 0309072697 (hardcover, 300 pages). *[autism,se]*

113. ***Exiting Nirvana: A Daughter's Life with Autism*** by Clara Claiborne Park. (Little Brown & Company, 2001). Foreword by Oliver Sacks. Continues the authors' story about her daughter. ISBN: 0316691178 (hardcover, 225 pages); ISBN: 0316691240 (paperback, 240 pages, Back Bay Books, 2002).*[autism,account]*

114. ***Enabling Communication in Children with Autism*** by Carol Potter & Chris Whittaker. (Jessica Kingsley Pub, 2001). ISBN: 1853029564 (paperback, 160 pages). *[autism,se,account]*

115. ***The Civil Wars of Jonah Moran*** by Marjorie Reynolds. (Berkley Pub Group, 2001). ISBN:

042517834X (paperback, 327 pages). *[autism,aspergers,fiction]*

116. ***Autism: The Search for Coherence*** by John Richer, editor & Sheila Coates, editor. (2001). ISBN: 1853028886 (paperback). *[autism]*

117. ***Clay*** by Colby F. Rodowsky. (Farrar Straus & Giroux, 2001). ISBN: 0374313385 (hardcover, 176 pages); ISBN: 0060006188 (paperback, 160 pages, HarperTrophy, 2004). *[autism,fiction,children]*

118. ***Beyond the Wall: Personal Experiences with Autism*** by Stephen Shore. (Autism Asperger Publishing Co, 2000). Autobiography. http://www.asperger.net ISBN: 0967251486 (paperback, 174 pages); ISBN: 1931282005 (paperback, 174 pages, Autism Asperger Publishing Co, 2001);ISBN: 1931282196 (paperback, 242 pages, Autism Asperger Publishing Co, 2002). *[autism,aspergers,account]*

119. ***Autism: A Holistic Approach*** by Bob Woodward & Marga Hogenboom. (Floris Books, 2001). Foreword

by Colwyn Trevarthen. ISBN: 0863153119 (paperback). *[autism,se]*

120. ***Understanding Other Minds; Perspectives from Developmental Cognitive Neuroscience, 2nd ed*** by Simon Baron-Cohen, Helen Tager-Flusberg & Donald Cohen. (Oxford University Press, 2000). http://www.oup.co.uk/isbn/0-19-852445-5 ISBN: 0198524463 (hardcover); ISBN: 0198524455 (paperback, 530 pages). *[autism]*

121. ***Separating, Losing and Excluding Children: Narratives of Difference*** by Tom Billington. (Falmer Pr, 2000). ISBN: 0415230888 (hardcover, 192 pages); ISBN: 0415230896 (hardcover, 192 pages). *[autism,account,se]*

122. ***Behavioral Concerns and Autistic Spectrum Disorders: Explorations and Strategies for Change*** by John Clements & Ewa Zarkowska. (Jessica Kingsley Pub, 2000). http://www.jkp.com/catalogue/autism/cle_beh.html ISBN: 1853027421 (paperback, 288 pages). *[autism]*

123. ***Autism in the Early Years: A Practical Guide*** by Val Cumine, Julia Leach & Gill Stevenson. (David Fulton, 2000). Part of the series *Resource Materials for Teachers*. http://www.independence.co.uk/bd.cgi/fulton/isb?1853465992 ISBN: 1853465992 (paperback). *[autism]*

124. ***What Does It Mean to Me?*** by Catherine Faherty. (Future Horizons, 2000). ISBN: 1885477597 (spiral-bound, 301 pages). *[autism, aspergers]*

125. ***Not Otherwise Specified: When Sensory Integration Affects Your Child: Working With the Child With Pervasive Developmental Disorder*** by Joan Fallon & Helene Fiorentino, editor. (Laredo Pub, 2000). The author is a Fellow of the International Council on Chiropractic Pediatrics. ISBN: 1564922863 (paperback, 96 pages). *[autism]*

126. ***Eating an Artichoke: A Mother's Perspective on Asperger Syndrome*** by Echo R. Fling. (London: Jessica Kingsley, 2000). About her son, Jimmy. Foreword by Tony

Attwood. http://www.jkp.com/catalogue/autism/fli_e at.html ISBN: 1853027111 (paperback, 200 pages). *[autism,aspergers,account]*

127. ***The Biology of the Autistic Syndromes, 3rd edition*** by Christopher Gillberg. (Cambridge University Press, 2000). Part of the series *Clincs in Developmental Medicine*. ISBN: 1898683220 (hardcover). *[autism,text]*

128. ***Autism A New Understanding!*** by Gail I Gillingham. (Tacit Publishing, Inc., 2000). ISBN: 0968786316 (paperback, 191 pages). *[autism]*

129. ***International Review of Research in Mental Retardation: Autism*** by Laraine Masters Glidden. (Academic Press, 2000). Part of the series*International Review of Research in Mental Retardation*. Volume 23 in the series. http://www.apcatalog.com/cgi-bin/AP?ISBN=0123662230&LOCATION=US&FORM=FORM2 ISBN: 0123662230 (hardcover, 320 pages). *[autism]*

130. ***New Social Stories: Illustrated Edition, 2nd edition*** by Carol Gray. (Future Horizons, 2000). ISBN: 188547766X (paperback, 120 pages). *[autism,social,se]*

131. ***Bringing Up a Challenging Child at Home: When Love is Not Enough*** by Jane Gregory. (London: Jessica Kingsley Publishers, 2000).http://www.jkp.com/catalogue/autism/gre_bri.html ISBN: 1853028746 (paperback, 192 pages). *[disability,account]*

132. ***The Gluten-Free Gourmet: Living Well without Wheat, 2nd ed*** by Bette Hagman. (Henry Holt, 2000). New edition. ISBN: 0805064842 (paperback, 272 pages). *[disability,nutrition]*

133. ***Asperger Syndrome, the Universe and Everything*** by Kenneth Hall. (London: Jessica Kingsley, 2000). Forewords by Ken P. Kerr and Gill Rowley. The author has Asperger Syndrome. ISBN: 1853029300 (112 pages). *[autism,aspergers,account]*

134. ***Facing Autism: Giving Parents Reasons for Hope, Encouragement for parents, Guidance for Help*** by Lynn M. Hamilton. (2000). ISBN: 1578562627 (paperback, 320 pages). *[autism,parent]*

135. ***Preschool Education Programs for Children with Autism, 2nd ed*** by Sandra L. Harris, ed & Jan S. Handleman, ed. (2000). ISBN: 0890798508 (paperback). *[autism,se,preschool]*

136. ***Autism in History: The Case of Hugh Blair of Borgue C. 1708-1765*** by Rab A. Houston & Uta Frith. (Blackwell Pub, 2000). Examination of Hugh Blair, eighteenth century Scottish landowner who appears to have been autistic. ISBN: 0631220887 (hardcover, 224 pages); ISBN: 0631220895 (paperback, 224 pages). *[autism,account]*

137. ***Autism: A Sensorimotor Approach to Management*** by Ruth A. Huebner. (Aspen Publishers, 2000). ISBN: 0834216450 (hardcover, 493 pages).*[autism,si]*

138. ***Reaching the Young Autistic Child: Reclaiming Non-Autistic Potential through Communicative***

Strategies and Games by Sibylle Janert. (London: Free Association Books, 2000). http://www.fab.com/Specfeat.htm ISBN: 1853434981 (paperback, 200 pages). *[autism]*

139.***The ABC's of Autism*** by M. Davi Kathiresan. (Autism Society of Michigan, 2000). I think it is suitable for children though by description it is meant for adults too. ISBN: 0970148003 (paperback, 31 pages). *[autism]*

140.***Asperger Syndrome*** by Ami Klin, editor, Fred R. Volkmar, editor & Sara S. Sparrow, editor. (Guilford Press, 2000). ISBN: 1572305347 (hardcover, 462 pages). *[autism,aspergers]*

141.***Diagnosing Jefferson*** by Norm Ledgin. (Future Horizons, 2000). http://www.diagnosingjefferson.com/ ISBN: 1885477600 (hardcover, 254 pages). *[autism,aspergers,account]*

142.***Celiac Disease: Methods and Protocols*** by Michael N. Marsh. (Humana Press, 2000). Part of the series *Methods in Molecular Medicine*. ISBN: 0896036502 (hardcover, 304 pages). *[allergy]*

143. ***Dear Charlie - A Grandfather's Love Letter to his Grandson with Autism*** by Earle P. Martin, Jr.. (Future Horizons, 2000). ISBN: 1885477619 (paperback, 156 pages). *[autism,family]*

144. ***The Self-Help Guide for Special Kids and their Parents*** by Joan Lord Matthews & James Williams. (Jessica Kingsley Pub, 2000). James Williams is the autistic son of Joan Matthews. The book includes approaches they worked out to his challenges. http://www.jkp/com/catalogue/autism/mat_sel.html ISBN: 1853029149 (paperback, 240 pages). *[autism]*

145. ***Practical Ideas That Really Work for Students With Autism Spectrum Disorders*** by Kathleen McConnell & Gail Ryser. (Pro Ed, 2000). ISBN: 0890798583 . *[autism,se]*

146. ***A Place Within the Sphere*** by Tanis Morran. (Trafford publishing, 2000). http://www.trafford.com/robots/00-0091.html

ISBN: 1552124266 (paperback, 194 pages). *[autism,fiction]*

147. ***Beyond the Silence: My Life, The World, and Autism*** by Tito R. Mukhopadhyay. (National Autistic Society, 2000). http://www.oneworld.org/autism_uk/publs/cata3.html ISBN: 1899280316 (paperback, 112 pages). *[autism,account]*

148. ***Exploring the Spectrum of Autism and Pervasive Developmental Disorders: Intervention Strategies*** by Carolyn Murray-Slutsky & Betty Paris. (Therapy Skill Builders, 2000). ISBN: 076165500X (paperback,). *[autism,treatment]*

149. ***Asperger Syndrome and Sensory Issues: Practical Solutions for Making Sense of the World*** by Brenda Smith Myles, Katherine Tapscott Cook, Nancy E. Miller, Luann Rinner & Lisa A. Robbins. (Autism Asperger Publishing Company, 2000). ISBN: 0967251478 (paperback, 129 pages, 2002). *[autism,aspergers,se]*

150. ***The Autism Handbook*** by National Autistic Society. (National Autistic Society, 2000). http://www.oneworld.org/autism_uk/publs/cata.html ISBN: 1899280243 (paperback, 200 pages). *[autism]*

151. ***Helping Children With Autism to Learn*** by Stuart Powell, editor. (David Fulton, 2000). http://www.independence.co.uk/bd.cgi/fulton/isb?1853466379 ISBN: 1853466379 (paperback). *[autism,se]*

152. ***Children with Autism: A Parent's Guide, 2nd edition*** by Michael D. Powers, ed. (Woodbine House, 2000). Part of the series *The Special Needs Collection*. Forward by Temple Grandin. See also description of first edition. http://www.woodbinehouse.com/cwa.html ISBN: 1890627046 (paperback, 375 pages). *[autism,parent,intro]*

153. ***Do-Watch-Listen-Say: Social and Communication Intervention for Children With Autism*** by Kathleen Ann Quill. (Paul H Brookes Pub,

2000).http://www.pbrookes.com/e-catalog/books/quill-4536/index.htm ISBN: 1557664536 (paperback, 448 pages). *[autism,se,social]*

154. ***Pervasive Developmental Disorder: An Altered Perspective*** by Barbara Quinn & Anthony Malone. (London: Jessica Kingsley Publishers, 2000).http://www.jkp.com/catalogue/autism/qui_per.html ISBN: 1853028762 (paperback, 144 pages). *[autism,pdd]*

155. ***Growing Up Severely Autistic: They Call Me Gabriel*** by Kate Rankin. (Jessica Kingsely Pub, 2000). http://www.jkp.com/catalogue/autism/ran_gro.htmlISBN: 1853028916 (paperback, 176 pages). *[autism,account]*

156. ***The Truth Out There*** by Celia Rees. (DK Publishing, 2000). Ages 9-12. ISBN: 0789426684 (hardcover, 240 pages). *[autism,aspergers,children,fiction]*

157. ***Raising a Child with Autism: A Guide to Applied Behavior Analysis for Parents*** by Shira Richman. (Jessica Kingsley, 2000). ISBN: 1853029106 (paperback, 160 pages). *[autism, behavioral]*

158. ***Coping When a Brother or Sister Is Autistic*** by Marsha Sarah Rosenberg. (Rosen Publishing Group, 2000). Part of the series *Coping*. ISBN: 0823931943 (hardcover). *[autism, family]*

159. ***The Martian in the Playground: Understanding the Schoolchild with Asperger's Syndrome*** by Clare Sainsbury. (Bristol: Lucky Duck Publishing Ltd., 2000). http://www.luckyduck.co.uk/ Selected in 2000 for UK's NASEN (National Association of Special Educational Needs) Academic Book Award. ISBN: 1873942087 . *[autism, aspergers, account]*

160. ***Making Visual Supports Work in the Home and Community: Strategies for Individuals with Autism and Asperger Syndrome*** by Jennifer Savner & Brenda Smith Myles. (Autism Asperger Publishing Company,

2000). http://www.asperger.net/visulbok.htm ISBN: 096725146X (spiral-bound, 40 pages).
[autism,aspergers]

161. ***Unraveling the Mystery of Autism and Pervasive Developmental Disorder: A Mother's Story of Research and Recovery*** by Karyn Seroussi. (Simon & Schuster, 2000). http://www.simonandschuster.com/book/default_book.cfm?isbn=0684831643 ISBN: 0684831643 (hardcover, 224 pages); ISBN: 0767907981 (paperback, 304 pages, Broadway Books, 2002). *[autism,account,allergy]*

162. ***Fragile Success: Nine Autistic Children, Childhood to Adulthood, 2nd Ed*** by Virginia Walker Sperry & Sally Provence. (Paul H. Brookes Pub Co., 2000). Traces their lives for over 30 years. http://www.pbrookes.com/e-catalog/books/sperry-4587/index.htm ISBN: 1557664587 (paperback, 304 pages).
[autism,account]

163. ***Learning to Live With High Functioning Autism: A Parent's Guide for Professionals*** by Mike Stanton. (Jessica Kingsley Pub, 2000). Written by a parent with professionals in mind. http://www.jkp.com/catalogue/autism/sta_lea.html ISBN: 1853029157 (paperback, 128 pages). *[autism,aspergers,account]*

164. ***Too Wise To Be Mistaken, Too Good To Be Unkind: Christian Parents Contend With Autism*** by Cathy Steere. (Grace and Truth Books, 2000).http://www.graceandtruthbooks.com/ ISBN: 1930133006 (paperback, 192 pages); ISBN: 1930133030 (paperback, 253 pages, Grace and Truth Books, 2005). *[autism,account,religious]*

165. ***I Am Special: Introducing Children and Young People to Their Autism Spectrum Disorder*** by Peter Vermeulen. (Jessica Kingsley Pub, 2000).http://www.jkp.com/catalogue/autism/ver_iam.html ISBN: 1853029165 (paperback, 240 pages). *[autism,children]*

166.***Autism Spectrum Disorders: A Transactional Developmental Perspective*** by Amy M. Wetherby, ed & Barry M. Prizant, ed. (Paul H. Brookes, 2000). Part of the series *Communication and Language Intervention*. Volume 9 in series. http://www.pbrookes.com/e-catalog/books/wetherby-4455/index.htm ISBN: 1557664455 (hardcover, 432 pages). *[autism]*

BIBLIOGRAPHY

~~~~~~~~~~~~~~~~~~~~~~~~~~

Able-Boone, H., & Sandall, S. (1990). An informed, family-centered approach to Public Law 99-457: Parental views. *Topics in Early Childhood Special Education*, 10, 100-111.

Aman, Michael G.; Lam, Kristen S.L.; Collier-Crespin, Angie (2003). Prevalence and Patterns of Use of Psychoactive Medicines among Individuals with Autism in the Autism Society of Ohio. *Journal of Autism & Developmental Disorders*, Vol. 33, 5, p527, 8p.

Aman, M.G., Van Bourgondein, M.E., Wolford, P.C. & Sarphare, G. (1995) Psychotropic and anticonvulsant drugs in subjects with autism: Prevalence and patterns of use. *Journal of the American Academy of Child and Adolescent Psychiatry*, 34, 1672-1681

Autism Society of America (2004). *Treatment Options*. Retrieved August 8, 2004 from http://www.autism-society.org/site/PageServer?pagename=TreatmentOptions

Barnett, W.S. (1995). *Long-Term Effects of Early Childhood Programs on Cognitive and School Outcomes.* The Future of Children, 5, 3, pp. 1-17

Bauer, S. (1995). Autism and the Pervasive Developmental Disorders: Part 1. *Pediatrics in Review.* 16, 4, pp. 130-136

Bauer, S. (1995). Autism and the Pervasive Developmental Disorders: Part 2. *Pediatrics in Review.* 16, 5, pp. 168-177

Baxter, Christine; Cummins, Robert A.; Yiolitis, Lewi. (2000), Parental stress attributed to family members with and without disability: A longitudinal study. *Journal of Intellectual & Developmental Disability,* Vol. 25 Issue 2, p105, 14p.

Brannan, C., Heflinger, E. and Foster (2003) The role of caregiver strain and other family variables in determining children's use of mental health services. *Journal of Emotional and Behavioral Disorders*

Bregman JD, Gerdtz J.(1997) Behavioral interventions.

Handbook of Autism and Pervasive Developmental Disorders. 2nd Ed. New York, NY: Wiley & Sons; 1997:606-630

DeMeyer, M. (1979). *Parents and children in Autism.* New York: John Wiley & Sons.

Diagnostic and Statistical Manual of Mental Disorders – Fourth Edition - TR. (2001) Washington, DC: American Psychiatric Association.

Digest of Education Statistics (2003). U.S. Department of Education, Office of Special Education Programs, Data Analysis system (DANS)

Fisman, S., Wolf, L., & Noh, S. (1989) Marital intimacy in parents of exceptional children. *Canadian Journal of Psychiatry*, 34, 519-525.

Guralnick, M.J, MD. (1997) *The Effectiveness of Early Intervention.* Baltimore, MD. : Paul H. Brooks Inc.

Heller, T., Miller, A., & Hsieh, K. (1999). Impact of a consumer-directed family support program on adults with developmental disabilities and their family caregivers. *Family Relations*, 48, 419-427.

Kaplan, M. (1994). *Role of vision in autism*. Paper presented at the Geneva Centre Symposium, Toronto, Canada

Klinger, LGA and Dawson, G. (1996) Autistic Disorder. In: *Child Psychology* (Eds. E.J. Mash and R.A. Barkley). The Guilford Press, New York

Koegel, R., Schreibman, L., Loos, L., Dirlich-Wilhelm, H., Dunlap, G., Robbins, F., & Plienis, A. Consistent stress profiles in mothers of children with autism. *Journal of Autism and Developmental Disorders*, 1992, 22, 205-216.

Individuals with Disabilities Education Act (2002) US Department of Education Statistics; Washington, DC

Individuals With Disabilities Education Act. (1997). US Department of Education Statistics; Washington, DC: Pub L No. 105-17

Lilly-J.D; Reed-D; Wheeler-K.G (2003). Perceptions of psychological contract violations in school districts that serve children with autism spectrum disorder: an exploratory qualitative study. *Journal-of-Applied-School-Psychology.* 20(1): 27-45,

Lovaas, O.I. (1979). Contrasting Illness and Behavioral Models for the Treatment of Autistic Children: A Historical Perspective. *Journal of Autism and Developmental Disorders.* 9,4, pp. 315-323.

Lovaas O, I. (1987) Behavioral treatment and normal educational and intellectual functioning in young autistic children. *Journal of Consulting Clinical Psychology.* Vol 55:3-9

McEachin JJ, Smith T, Lovaas O.I. (1993). Long-term outcome for children with autism who received early intensive behavioral treatment. American Journal of Mental Retardation, Vol.97: 359-372

Moroz, K.J. (1989). Educating Autistic Children and Youths: A School-Family-Community Partnership. (Winter 1989) *Social Work in Education*, 4, pp.107-124

Newsome, W.S. (2000) Parental perceptions during periods

of transition: implications for social workers serving families coping with autism. *Journal-of-Family-Social-Work.* 5(2): 17-31, 2000

Olsen, M.B. & Hwang, C.P. (2002) Sense of Coherence in Parents. *Journal of Intellectual Disability Research.* Volume 46 Part 7, 548-559.

Patterson, Joan M (May2002). Integrating Family Resilience and Family Stress Theory *Journal of Marriage & the Family,* Vol. 64, Issue 2

Powers, M. Psy.D. (1989). *Children with Autism – A Parents' Guide.* Rockville, MD: Woodbine House.

Rodrigue, J.R., Morgan, S.B., & Geoffken, G. Families of autistic children: Psychological functioning of mothers. *Journal of Clinical Psychology,* 1990, Vol. 19, 371-379.

Shannon, P. (2004). Barriers to family-centered services for infants and toddlers with developmental delays. *Social Work.* 49(2): 301-308.

Simpson, R.L. (1995). Individualized Education Programs

for Students with Autism: Including the Parents in the Process. *Focus on Autistic Behavior*, October 1995, 10, 4, p. 11-16

Stone, W. L.; Ousley, O. Y.; Hepburn, S. L.; Hogan, K. L.; Brown, C. S (1999). Patterns of adaptive behavior in very young children with autism; *American Journal on Mental Retardation;* p187-199, 13p.

Turbiville, Vicki P.; Marquis, Janet G. (2001). Father Participation in Early Education Programs. *Topics in Early Childhood Special Education*, Winter, Vol. 21 Issue 4, p223, 9p.

U.S Census Bureau – *U.S Department of Education Office of Special Education Programs Data Analysis Systems* (2000) Washington. DC.

Zeanah, C. (2000) (2nd ED) *Handbook on Infant Mental Health*. New York, NY; The Guilford Press.